THEMES
for early years

WATER

JENNY MORRIS

THEMES
for early years

Author Jenny Morris
Editor Libby Russell
Assistant editor Sally Gray
Series designer Lynne Joesbury
Designer Louise Belcher
Illustrations Louise Gardener
Cover Based on an illustration by Sue Coney
Action Rhymes, Poems and Stories compiled by Jackie Andrews
Songs compiled by Peter Morrell
Assemblies chapter by Lesley Prior
Thanks to Guy, Bruce, Thomas, Penelope and Madeline.

Designed using Aldus Pagemaker
Processed by Scholastic Ltd, Leamington Spa
Printed in Great Britain by Hartnolls Ltd., Bodmin

Published by Scholastic Ltd, Villiers House, Clarendon Avenue, Leamington Spa, Warwickshire CV32 5PR
© 1997 Scholastic Ltd   Text © 1997 Jenny Morris
1 2 3 4 5 6 7 8 9   7 8 9 0 1 2 3 4 5 6

The publishers gratefully acknowledge permission to reproduce the following copyright material:
Jackie Andrews for 'Jonah' © 1997; Clive Barnwell for 'One Little Drop of Water'; 'A Man With A Watering Can' and 'Terrors Of The Sea' © 1997;
Ann Bryant for the words and music to 'My Little Island' and 'What's That Bobbing In The Sea?' © 1997; Debbie Campbell for 'I Think Ice Is Nice' ©
1997; Coward-McCann Inc for 'When I Was Christened' by David McCord from *And What's More* © 1941, David McCord (Putnam Publishing); Gina
Douthwaite for 'The Shape of Water' © 1997; John Foster for 'The Central Heating' from *Ghost Poems* © 1990 (Oxford University Press); Lesley
Funge for 'A Rainy Day!' © 1997; Ladybird Books Ltd. for 'Indoor Sports' by Joan Stimson from *Storytime For 3 Year Olds* © 1988, Joan Stimson
(Ladybird Books Ltd.); Wendy Larmont for the poems 'Melting', 'Ice Lollies', 'Wet Playtime' and 'Bubbles' © 1997; Wes Magee for 'The Harbour Wall'
and 'The Waterfall' © 1997; Tony Mitton for 'Storm' © 1993 Tony Mitton, 'Washday' © 1997 Tony Mitton, 'Voices of Water' was first published in
Performance Poems ed. Brian Moses © 1996 Tony Mitton (Southgate); Peter Morrell for 'Hello Me!' © 1997; Judith Nicholls for 'Blue Wellies, Yellow
Wellies' and 'Bathtime' first published in *Popcorn Pie* by Judith Nicholls © 1988 (Mary Glasgow Press, now Collins Primary Poetry Pack 2) and Judith
Nicholls 'Water's For' from *Another Very First Poetry Book* compiled by John Foster © 1992 Judith Nicholls (Oxford University Press); Sue Palmer,
Language Live, Truro for 'Wake Up To A Riddle' © 1997 Sue Palmer; Gillian Parker for the words and music to 'Washday' © 1997; Jan Pollard for
'Days By The Sea' and 'Who Lives In The Sea?' © 1997; Lesley Prior for the three assemblies © 1997; John Rice for 'Park Pond' © 1997; The Watts
Group for 'Water' from *First Poems* by Lucy Coats © 1994 Lucy Coates (Orchard Books); Irene Yates for 'Ellie's Magic Roof Garden' © 1997.
Every effort has been made to trace copyright holders and the publishers apologise for any inadvertent omissions.

British Library Cataloguing-in-Publication Data A catalogue record for this book is available from the British Library.

ISBN 0-590-53464-8

The right of Jenny Morris to be identified as the Author of this work has been asserted by her in accordance with the Copyright,
Designs and Patents Act 1988.

CONTENTS

INTRODUCTION

Some group leaders may think that a water theme would be far too messy. After all, which leader hasn't gone to look for a missing child in the cloakroom, only to find a little group of children watching fascinated as the water flows out of the basin all over the floor? Fortunately there are many ways that children can learn about water without ending up with a scene reminiscent of the Sorcerer's Apprentice!

Children start learning about the nature and properties of water very early in their lives when they play with their toys in the bath. Once they have joined a playgroup, nursery or reception class they continue to play with water in the water tray. It is a very sociable activity as they interact and help each other with the practical aspects of water play. Water is relaxing, soothing and easy to handle and provides emotional pleasure and satisfaction as children learn to control it. They cannot fail when they play with water; they succeed, and this success maintains their interest and stimulates them to find out more. This book provides activities to satisfy their curiosity.

Over 70% of the earth's surface is covered with water. It is all around us in the sea, lakes, rivers and streams – it cannot run out. This book looks at the problem that water is not always in the right place, at the right time and in the right condition.

It explains that water is an essential element of life for all living plants and animals, including us. It shows how we depend on water everyday for drinking, washing, cooking, cleaning and growing our food. Finally it recognises that without water the world would dry up and become uninhabitable.

AIMS OF THE BOOK

Ideally children could learn about many of the aspects of water from first hand experience either at the seaside, by a stream or while pond-dipping. Unfortunately visits such as these are not always possible and present the group leader with a lot of organisation. However, learning about water need not rely on outside visits nor be restricted to a water tray.

Pouring, squirting and splashing water provides opportunities for scientific discoveries; moving and measuring water concerns mathematical concepts; becoming familiar with the different forms of water – solid (ice), liquid (water), or gas (steam) introduces new vocabulary. All these activities encourage language development.

This book approaches the topic of water in areas which are of most interest and relevance to young children. These are – Weather and Water; Sea Water; Fresh Water; Using Water at Home; Living Things Need Water; Working with Water.

HOW TO USE THIS BOOK

Water is a valuable resource and this book on 'Water' in the Themes for early years series, shows young children just how important it is. Using water to experiment and play with can get messy. This doesn't matter so much if you are working outside but you cannot always wait for warm sunny days. There are practical ways of keeping inside water activities under control. If your group doesn't have a water tray, then a baby bath or old galvanised tin bath will do just as well. Never, ever leave young children unsupervised while they are playing with water in these containers. Cover the floor where you are working with a ground sheet which is less slippery than polythene sheeting. Keep dishcloths, sponges and a squeegee mop and bucket readily available, and teach the children to mop up any spills as they happen and before they become a danger. You can make water aprons easily out of plastic coated fabric and Velcro, but under strict supervision dustbin liners with holes cut for head and arms are a good substitute. The activities in this book use a variety of resources which behave differently with water. Many of these resources can be found in camping, gardening, pet, wine-making and hardware shops.

Inevitably there will be at least one child who is very anxious about getting wet. Provide warm water for this child, it is more gentle and comfortable than plunging hands into cold water.

TOPIC WEB

This is a practical way of seeing how the water theme covers the preparation of all the subjects of the National Curriculum: Maths, English, Science, Design and Technology, Music, Art, Physical Education, Geography, History, the Scottish 5–14 Guidelines and Religious Education. The topic web can be photocopied and used as a check list for your planning.

ACTIVITY PAGES

There are six chapters in this book each of which covers a different aspect of water. Each chapter has eight activity pages which follow the same format, focusing on one main Water activity and with 'objectives' which prepare for a National Curriculum / Scottish Guidelines subject.

The 'group size' which is indicated is merely a suggestion but this can obviously vary according to your premises, time and the adult to child ratio.

'Preparation' for activities has been kept to a minimum and you may find that the children themselves are able to help with this. This could involve making or setting out equipment. Alternatively, the children may need prior experience or knowledge which is essential to the success of the activity.

'What you need' acts like the ingredients listed for a recipe. If you are short of any item it may well

ASSEMBLIES

Your group may be multi-cultural and have different forms of worship. These can be shared and experienced during assembly or sharing time, incorporating recognition of the universal need for water.

RESOURCES SECTION

This includes stories, poems, rhymes and songs based on the Water theme. They have been compiled for the convenience of making the book self-contained and can be used with the activity pages or in their own right. You may photocopy them for ease of use.

PHOTOCOPIABLE ACTIVITY SHEETS

These eight pages of games and activities can be photocopied. They have been specially devised to enhance specific activity pages. Many can be adapted to be used in other ways such as for hand-writing practice or for learning new vocabulary.

RECOMMENDED MATERIALS

This section refers to information and resource books, some of which have been used throughout this book. It also lists additional music, poetry, stories and equipment which would make a useful contribution to the theme of Water.

spoil the end result so it is advisable to gather everything before you start. The children will enjoy helping to collect items from home or within your group. If the children know what they are going to be doing it stimulates their interest and initiates keen anticipation.

'What you do' and the 'Discussion' are inter-dependent and it is not intended that these two sections should be dealt with separately. You will often be talking about what you are doing and questioning the children while they are completing the activity.

The 'Follow-up activities' are extensions of the same activity, or cross-curricula ideas for further work relating to the activity. They can be done at any time and may fit in with other activity pages.

The activities have been grouped in chapters but they can be done in any order. Use this book in the way that is most enjoyable and convenient for you and your group of children. Be open to the children's suggestions, share in their experiences and they will reward you with originality and true self-expression.

DISPLAYS

There are five separate displays described in this chapter which draw together ideas from different Water activity pages. Displays are a good way of instilling group co-operation and of recording children's work for you and for them. It is worth taking care in planning and labelling displays so that they can be used for observation, talking about, reading and enjoying.

EXPRESSIVE ARTS

Planning towards the National Curriculum and the Scottish National guidelines 5-14

THEMES
for early years

MATHEMATICS

ENVIRONMENTAL STUDIES

SCIENCE

DESIGN AND TECHNOLOGY

HISTORY/PEOPLE IN THE PAST

GEOGRAPHY/PEOPLE AND PLACE

PHOTOCOPIABLE

PREPARING FOR PRIMARY SCHOOL

THE NATIONAL CURRICULUM

To ensure that all children between the ages of five and sixteen in England and Wales cover a wide range of subjects in State Schools the government has introduced the National Curriculum. This means that when children start compulsory education at five years old it is certain that they will be covering the same areas of the curriculum, for the same amount of time each week as a child in any other State School in the country.

The National Curriculum subjects are Mathematics, English, Science, Geography, History, Design and Technology, Art, Music, PE, Information Technology and RE. The programmes of study give guidance to teachers of what should be taught in each subject. Children's progress is assessed at the end of Year Two (when they are six or seven) by Standard Assessment Tasks and the teacher's personal judgement.

Although the National Curriculum does not involve pre-school children it would seem wise to give them a thorough grounding in the subjects which they will soon be meeting.

This book sets out to give such a grounding based around the theme of Water. The children will

be involved in physically copying the arching movement of water jets, experimenting on extracting salt from salt-water and discovering how to find a puncture in a tyre. All the activities have clear learning objectives which link in to relevant National Curriculum subject areas and will provide children with a firm foundation for their further education. The topic web on pages 8 and 9 shows the division of subject areas and activities.

The activities also fit well into the six areas of Learning for under fives recommended by the School Curriculum and Assessment Authority in the document *Nursery Education: Desirable Outcomes for Children's Learning on entering Compulsory Education.*

THE SCOTTISH 5–14 NATIONAL GUIDELINES

In Scotland there are National Guidelines for schools on what should be taught to children between the ages of five and fourteen.

These National Guidelines are divided into six main curriculum areas: English Language, Mathematics, Environmental studies, Expressive arts, Religious and moral education, Personal and social development.

Within these main areas further subjects are found, for example 'Expressive arts' includes art and design, drama, music and PE. Strands are also identified within each subject, for example Maths includes problem-solving and enquiry, and shape, position and movement.

Most nurseries and playgroups will find that the experiences they are already offering children will be laying a good foundation for this curriculum. This book provides activities which have been specially written to prepare for many aspects of it, and they will also fit well into the pre-school curriculum guidelines issued by local authorities throughout Scotland.

To help with planning, the individual activities have been allocated to separate areas of the curriculum on the topic web on pages 8 and 9. The children's personal and social development is an on-going theme that is incorporated throughout the activities in the book.

CHAPTER 1
WEATHER AND WATER

In Britain our everyday lives are very much governed by the weather because it varies so much. Clouds, rain, storms, sleet, snow, floods, fog, frost, drizzle, dew and mist all involve water in one form or another. This chapter looks at these different forms of water.

INVISIBLE DROPS

Objective

Science — To demonstrate that water is present in the air and can be seen when it becomes cold.

Group size

Six children.

What you need

Three mirrors — one per pair of children, a smudgy pair of spectacles, a paper towel.

What to do

Organise the children into pairs, give each pair a mirror and ask them to look at their reflections. They can take turns to breathe hard on to the mirror and find out if they can still see themselves. Take the smudgy spectacles and ask the children how they can be cleaned without using water. Breathe hard on to them and clean them with a paper towel. Show them to the children.

Discussion

The air is full of tiny droplets of water so small you cannot see them. These droplets will show when they touch something cold. Have the children noticed how the bathroom steams up when they have a bath on a very cold evening? Could the children see themselves clearly when they breathed hard on to the mirror? Their breath contains water droplets which showed up when they hit the cold mirror. Why did breathing on the spectacles make them easier to clean (it provided moisture).

Follow-up activities

✧ Boil a pan of water and watch the windows steam up. Write your name with your finger on the window. (Alternatively, this could be done on a cold day when the windows are already steamed up.)
✧ Water a pot plant and enclose it in a polythene bag. After a few hours check the sides of the polythene bag and see the water drops. The plant has 'breathed' and the water droplets show on the bag.
✧ Wash some dolls' clothes. Hang them up to dry and guess where all the wet goes.
✧ Sing the song 'One Little Drop of Water' on page 84.

DARK CLOUDS

* *

Objective

Geography – To find out where rain comes from and to play a game of matching weather symbols.

Group size

Six children.

What you need

Five copies of photocopiable sheet 88, scissors or paper cutter, copy of a newspaper weather report.

Preparation

Stick five copies of sheet 88 to thin card (or photocopy directly on to card) and cut up four copies into the six symbols to make 24 cards. Shuffle the cards. Leave the fifth copy uncut.

What to do

Show the children the six weather symbols on the uncut card and ask them where they have seen them before (T.V.). Turn to the weather forecast in the newspaper and point out the types of symbols used. Find out who knows what each symbol represents and ask them to explain to the others. Sit the children round a table for the card game. Give them a few cards each to place face down in front of them. Take turns to try and match a pair of symbols by turning over any two cards.

If the two cards match pick them up and keep the pair. If they don't match they must be turned over again. The children have to try and remember what has been turned over so they can match more cards. The game is finished when all the pairs are matched.

Discussion

Rain falls from big, dark clouds and collects in rivers which flow into the sea. This is where we get most of our water from (other collectors of water include reservoirs which are also used as a source of water). If it doesn't rain the rivers dry up and we are then short of water to use. Weather forecasts tell us when it is going to rain. Why is it especially important for farmers and gardeners to know when it will rain? (Because crops won't grow without rain.)

Follow-up activities

✧ Ask the children to watch a weather forecast on the television at home. Pin up a map of the British Isles and role-play the forecaster. Stick the weather symbols on to the map using Blu-Tack.
✧ Make a 'bottle octave'. Add different amounts of water to eight milk bottles and tap them with a spoon to make the notes of a musical scale.
✧ Leave eight different shaped glass containers in the same place outside when it next rains. Compare the different water levels and then use these to make varying notes.
✧ Look at a globe or map of the world and find the large patches of blue sea and strips of blue rivers.
✧ Say the poem 'Storm' on page 73.

RAINDROPS

Objective

English – To listen to sentences about the weather and see if they make sense.

Group size

The whole group.

What you need

Props or pictures that will go with the sentences below – for example: swimming costume or trunks, sledge, pair of shorts, kite, slippers, wellington boots, umbrella. Some silly sentences such as these:-

• When it rains I need to put on my swimming costume before I go out.
• I love hot days when I can ride on my sledge to the shops.
• It is very cold today so Mum told me to wear my shorts.
• There's no wind this morning so I'm going to fly my kite on the hill.
• Dad says I must wear my bedroom slippers if I want to splash in the puddles.
• Gran said that if it is sunny we should take our umbrellas with us.

What to do

Select the appropriate prop and say the sentences one at a time to the children. See what their reaction is. Give them time after each sentence to say whether they think it makes sense. If they think it's silly then ask them to explain why. Let them change the prop for the one that should go with the sentence to make sense. Ask them to say this new sensible sentence.

Discussion

The things we do and the clothes we wear are governed by weather conditions. What kind of clothes do we wear on hot, windy, cold and rainy days? Explain to the children what waterproof means. How do animals manage in the rain? When it's raining why do we say it's nice weather for ducks? Have any of the children ever been caught out in the rain? Did they get soaked to the skin? What words can they think of to describe rain? (Pouring, wet, trickle, drizzle, soaking.)

Follow-up activities

✧ Watch raindrops trickle down the window pane. Notice the pattern they make and draw or paint this on paper.
✧ With a glockenspiel or chime bars let the children make the sounds of raindrops falling. Vary the intensity for light or heavy raindrops.
✧ Lay newspaper sheets on the floor and play a game of jumping over 'puddles'.
✧ Drip a drop of water onto a printed word. What happens? (Magnifies.)
✧ Say the poem 'Wet Playtime' and the action rhyme 'Rain' on pages 71 and 72.
✧ Sing the song 'A Rainy Day' on page 83.
✧ Make a rainy day display (see page 63).

THE RAINY SEASON

Objective

Geography – To discover that houses are built in different ways according to where they are in the world and to make a 'house' on stilts.

Group size

Six children.

What you need

A variety of construction toys including those with plastic bricks, large washing up bowl or the water tray, watering can with a perforated end cap and full of water, picture of a clown on stilts.

What to do

The children can work in pairs if they understand about sharing and helping each other. Show them the picture of the clown and point out how the stilts raise him above the ground. Ask the children to use the construction toys to build a house and four towers which can be used as stilts. Place the house on the stilts (towers) so it is raised like the clown. Put the raised houses in the empty washing up bowl or water tray. Pour on the 'rain' out of the watering can and let the children watch how the water level rises and yet the insides of their houses keep dry.

Discussion

People who live in the British Isles are used to having four seasons in the year. Can the children name these seasons? Explain that in some other parts of the world countries only have two seasons – a rainy season and a dry season. How do people who live in places where there is a rainy season stop their houses from becoming flooded? In what way do these people visit each other's houses or go shopping and how do the children get to school? (Some go by boat.) Rice grows very well in countries with a rainy season. Rice plants like to have their 'feet' wet and grow best in flooded fields.

Follow-up activities

◇ Make a collection of different types of rice, compare their colour and size.
◇ Use the construction sets to make a flat-bottomed boat that could be used in the rainy season.
◇ Read the story 'Wake up to a Riddle' on page 76.

NOAH'S RAINBOW

Objective

Religious Education — To think about the symbol of the rainbow in the story of Noah's Ark and to make a rainbow picture.

Group size

Six children.

What you need

The story of Noah's Ark (The Lion Storyteller Bible 1995), picture of a rainbow, six pieces of A4 sized paper with the faint outline of a rainbow drawn on, set of water soluble crayons, pastels or chalks which include the seven colours of the rainbow (red, orange, yellow, green, blue, indigo, violet), two thick clean paint brushes, two water pots.

Preparation

Draw and copy the rainbow outlines.

What to do

Read the story of Noah's Ark and show the children the picture of a rainbow. Explain that it is a sign that there will never be such a terrible flood again. Give them each a copy of the rainbow outline to create their own picture. Hold up each of the seven crayons in turn and see who knows the names of the colours. Let the children share the crayons as they colour in each band on their rainbow outline in the correct order (see below). When they have finished show them how to brush over their rainbow with a damp paintbrush, or smudge the chalks with a finger-tip (following the curves of the rainbow). All the colours will blend into each other like a real rainbow.

Discussion

A rainbow is a huge coloured curve in the sky. Do the children know when rainbows appear? (When the sun shines through drops of water — especially when it's raining.) The colours of a rainbow have a special order which is always the same no matter where it is seen in the world. Do they know what this order is? (From the inner curve out: red, orange, yellow, green, blue, indigo, violet — indigo is deep blue.)

Follow-up activities

✧ Colour seven sections of a circle of card (about 8cm diameter) with the rainbow colours. Push a pencil through a hole in the centre and spin the rainbow wheel.

✧ If it is practicable, make your own rainbow outside. Stand with your back to the sun and spray water from a hose-pipe. Look carefully and you will see a rainbow.

✧ Say the rhyme (mnemonic) 'Richard Of York Gained Battles In Vain'. The initial sound of each word is the same as the initial sound of the names of the rainbow colours. For example: Richard/red, Of/orange and so on.

✧ Make a group survey of favourite colours. Which is the most popular colour?

✧ Add a rainbow to the display 'Rain Rain Go Away' on page 63.

JUNGLE BOTTLE

Objective

Design and Technology — To design and use tools for growing plants in a bottle which will create the humid conditions of a rain forest.

Group size

Six children.

What you need

A large clean bottle or jar with lid (tall plastic sweet jar), pebbles (from a garden centre), bag of all purpose (peat-free) compost, four very small slow growing plants suitable for humid conditions such as: aluminium plant, small palm, peperomia, croton, begonia, slow-growing ivy, maidenhair fern. Jug of water, plastic funnel, 30cm square of thin card, stapler, kitchen fork and teaspoon, empty cotton reel, three canes 30cm long, adhesive tape, pineapple, mango, avocado.

Preparation

Thoroughly dry enough compost to form a 7cm layer in the bottle.

What to do

Ask the children to think of ways to tip the pebbles and the compost into the mini-jungle jar without spilling them all over the place. Let them try the funnel. How can they make a wider funnel? Make an open-ended cone with the card and secure it with the stapler. Pour through enough pebbles to form a 3cm layer and then enough dry compost to form a 7cm layer.

Ask the children to suggest ways to make tools which can reach down inside the jar. If the spoon and fork do not reach what can they do? Tape canes to the spoon and fork and then use them to make holes in the soil for the plants.

Gently place the plants in the soil. Wedge the third cane into the cotton reel to tamp down the soil around the plants. Do not use too many plants as they will need room to grow.

Water your jungle sparingly through the plastic funnel and replace the lid. The jar may steam up at first but will soon clear. Place the bottle garden inside but not in full sun. It won't need much attention at all. Show and let the children touch the pineapple, mango and avocado as you go through the following discussion.

Discussion

Some hot places in the world have rain every day. In these hot damp jungle conditions, plants will grow all through the year and become enormous. There are millions of very tall trees which make up the rainforests. Pineapples, mangoes and avocados grow in the rain forest. What kinds of animals live in these tropical conditions? (Monkeys, snakes, parrots.)

Follow-up activities

◇ Move as if you were an animal trying to get through the jungle — climb, slither, crawl, jump, 'fly'.
◇ Soak an avocado stone for 24 hours, then rest it in the neck of a bottle touching water. Be patient and it will start to grow.
◇ Pull the leaves off the top of a pineapple (be careful of prickles), count them and arrange them in size order.
◇ Say the poem 'Rain' by Robert Louis Stevenson in a *Child's Garden of Verse* (Wordsworth).

WHO'S BEEN HERE?

Objective

Art – To print using various items which represent footprints in the snow.

Group size

Six children.

What you need

Play people, toy animals and birds with distinctive feet, Action Man boots, Sindy doll shoes, a dressmaker's tracing wheel, two large potatoes (optional – see below), mixed black powder paint, two damp sponges in two shallow bowls, a piece of thick white paper for each child.

Preparation

If you don't have suitable toy animals and birds you can make footprints out of halved potatoes. Experiment with the paint thickness to see what works best, add more paint or water as necessary.

What to do

Ensure that all the children are wearing painting overalls as this is a very messy activity! Pour some of the paint on to the damp sponges. Put several layers of newspaper under the white paper – this will improve the prints. Press one of the 'feet' on to the sponge and print it across the paper as if it had walked. Do the same with all the feet and the tracing wheel, which will look like a vehicle track.

Discussion

Sometimes when the weather is very cold, the water in the air freezes and falls to the ground as snowflakes. Snow makes everything look as though it has been covered by a thick white blanket. Ask who has seen snow before. Have they only seen it in pictures? Ask anyone who has ever seen real snow why everywhere sounds so quiet. (Snow stops the sound of things banging and clattering.) What sort of animals live in cold countries? (Polar bears, seals, penguins.) Can the children name some of the clothes they would wear in snowy weather? How many different activities could they do in the snow? (Build a snowman, throw snowballs, ski, toboggan, leave footprints.)

Follow-up activities

✧ After snow examine a snowflake through a magnifying glass and compare how it feels different to water. Collect some snow and weigh it. Leave it to melt on the scales. Does the weight change?
✧ Gather some broken-off bare tree branches and paint the top side with white paint to look like snow.
✧ Fold a circle (9cm diameter) of white paper in half, then into three (see diagram). Cut bits from the sides before opening it out into a snowflake.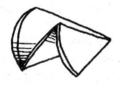
✧ Give each child a snowman outline and ask them to draw on one hat, one scarf, one nose, one mouth, two eyes, two twig arms and three large buttons.
✧ Sing 'Who saw the footprints in the snow?' from *Knock at the door* (Ward Lock) and say the poems 'Melting' on page 70 and 'Winter Morning' by Ogden Nash in *The Young Puffin Book of Verse*.

DON'T SLIP!

Objective

Physical Education — To practise balancing as if walking on icy ground.

Group size

Ten children.

What you need

Some ice-cubes, a bowl of water, smooth shiny table/tray surface, or the floor.

Preparation

Freeze some ice-cubes in advance.

What to do

Show the children that ice cubes are very slippery. Let them handle them and slide them across the shiny surface.

Ask them to pretend to walk on slippery, icy ground. Encourage them to put their arms out to help them balance. How long can they stay up before they fall down with a sudden bump? As they become more confident they could try ice 'skating' and sliding. It is very cold so they will need to move their hands and fingers to stop the cold from nipping them. Float the ice-cubes in the bowl of water and ask the children to bob around the room in the same way, occasionally clinking (not bashing!) into each other. Like the ice-cubes they will slowly start to melt. Gradually they can turn back into a solid block of ice by huddling together, as the bowl of melted cubes would if put into a freezer.

Discussion

When water gets very cold (below 0°C) it freezes and becomes hard. This solid water is called ice. Sometimes the top of a puddle freezes and turns into a thin ice lid. Have the children ever stamped on a puddle lid, made it splinter and heard it crack? Why isn't it safe to walk on a frozen pond? Is it safe to skate at an ice rink? Tiny moisture drops of morning dew turn into frost when the weather is freezing. Frost can cover everything outside in white. We pretend that it is the work of a person called Jack Frost. He makes patterns on windows and leaves, and makes spider's webs stand out as the frost follows the web's pattern.

Follow-up activities

✧ Give each child a copy of photocopiable page 89 to count the icy things. They can cut out each set of pictures and arrange them in numerical order.
✧ If there is a large enough freezer available, freeze a balloon full of water. Remove the rubber and float the ice in water like an iceberg. How much is under the water? (Ice floats because trapped air makes it lighter than water.)
✧ Salt some ice-cubes and compare their melting rate with unsalted cubes.
✧ Make ice lollies using different shaped containers such as thimbles or sterilised sand-moulds.
✧ Say the poem 'Ice Lollies' on page 74.
✧ Sing 'I think Ice is Nice' on page 85.
✧ Read the poem 'Jack Frost in the Garden' from *The Book of a Thousand Poems* (Collins).

CHAPTER 2
SEA WATER

'Water water everywhere nor any drop to drink' said Samuel T Coleridge.
In this chapter the children will be able to find out why they can't drink sea water.
They will also discover how the sea's power can separate land into islands and
wear away the edges of the coast.

WHERE'S IT GONE?

Objective

Science – To find out that some things disappear in water.

Group size

Six children.

What you need

A drinking glass, a saucer (not white) and a teaspoon for each child, 100g of cooking salt, jug of cold water.

What to do

Pour approximately 0.1 litre of water into each glass and give one to each child. Ask them to have a sip of water. Give each child a spoon to take a spoonful of salt and tip it into their glass of water (be careful of salt near eyes). Wait for a minute and observe what happens. Ask them to stir their glass of salt and water vigorously for about 15 seconds.

Leave it to stand and see what has happened after a minute. Lift the glass carefully and look through the bottom of the glass. Stir again vigorously. Dip a finger in the water and taste it.

Pour a little of the water from the glass into a saucer and leave it in a very warm place. The children can write their own name label to put by their saucer. When all the water has gone (this might take two days) chip off a bit of what's left on the saucer and taste it.

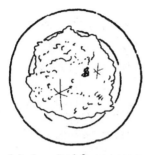

Salt deposits left on saucer after water has evaporated

Discussion

Did the sip of water taste of anything? What happened to the salt first, when it was tipped into the glass of water and then when the children stirred the water vigorously? What did the water on your finger taste like? When the water in the saucer had gone, what was left on the saucer? The sea is a large mass of salt water. Can we tell that the sea is salty just by looking at it? Could we drink sea water if we were thirsty?

Follow-up activities

◇ Repeat the experiment using a spoonful of sugar instead of salt.
◇ Try both the salt and sugar experiments using hot water. Is there any difference from when cold water was used?
◇ Use a magnifying glass to look at the remnants on the saucer when the water has dried up. Use chalk on black paper to draw the pattern that the salt left.
◇ Say 'She sells sea-shells on the sea-shore'.
◇ Make jellies to eat. Notice how the 'texture' of the water changes when the jelly has set.

DIPPING DIPS

Objective

Art – To finger paint a picture which will look like the movement of waves.

Group size

Two children at a time will be enough for this messy craft!

What you need

A piece of blue sugar paper (approximately 40 x 30cm) for each child, three pots of fairly thick ready mixed powder paint – one white, one dark blue and one light blue, a saucer for each paint colour, plenty of newspaper, a damp cloth.

What to do

With the children in their overalls show them how to point their index finger and dip their arm up and down (like waves) through the air. Place the blue sugar paper on top of some newspaper on a table. Pour a different coloured paint onto each saucer. Keep the white paint well out of the way until later. Ask the children to dip their index finger into the light blue paint first and 'brush' their finger up and down in a wave-like movement across the paper.

When they've painted enough light blue waves they can finger paint some dark blue waves mixing and blending them with the others. Finally, having wiped their fingers let them dip into the white paint to make the swirls on the top (crest) of the waves.

Discussion

When the wind blows it causes the sea water to dip up and down making waves. Even the slightest bit of wind will cause little ripples or wavelets. If it's very windy will the waves be big or small? When the waves are very high and topped with white we say the sea is very angry. If there are hardly any waves we say the sea is calm. Waves which have come from a long way away 'break' on to the beach and look like frothy white foam. When the tide is in (twice a day) the sea comes up the beach and when the tide goes out it leaves wavy lines in the sand.

Follow-up activities

✧ Cut some black paper into the shape of a boat (see diagram) and stick it on to the waves. Draw some sea birds above the waves using a thick black marker pen.
✧ Stretch out a long skipping rope and shake one end. What can you see moving along?
✧ Practise writing a row of deep waves (dips) and then use a crayon to pick out the 'w's (see diagram).

✧ Use the cardboard divider from an apple box and brush-paint the ridges in blue to look like waves.
✧ Read 'Days by the Sea' a poem on page 67.
✧ Fingerpaint some waves in the display 'Beside the Seaside' (see page 61).

BEACH PEBBLES

Objective

English — To play a game using pebbles to encourage recognition of the alphabet.

Group size

Five children.

What you need

Some small pebbles (for example, a shovel-full of 20mm single size pink gravel from a builder's merchant), round-tipped black marker pen, 26 pieces of stiff card (about 10cm square), bag to hold 26 pebbles.

Preparation

Wash and dry the pebbles. Write a lower case letter on to each of the 26 pebbles.

What to do

Let each child pick five letter pebbles from the bag (one will be left — leave the corresponding letter card out too) and arrange them in front of them so that they can see the letters. Now show the children one of the cards. Wait and see if anyone can say the sound of the letter. Ask them to look at their pebbles to see who has got the same one as on the card. Whoever has got the pebble gives it to you. Continue to show all the cards until all the pebbles have been given in. Encourage the children to help arrange the pebbles in alphabetical order. Does anyone know which letter is missing? Take it out of the bag and put it in its right place.

Discussion

Waves go backwards and forwards so many times that they start breaking rocks off the coast. These rocks are then moved backwards and forwards by the water and keep rubbing against each other until they get smaller and smaller. After a very long time (millions of years) they become smooth pebbles. Some beaches are covered in pebbles. What are pebbles called when they become tiny little grains? (Sand.) What kind of things do the waves leave on the beach? (Seaweed, shells, bits of wood, bottles with messages in.)

Follow-up activities

✧ Vary the pebble game by using capital letters and some consonant blends — sh, ch, wh, th.
✧ Make a pebble mat. Spread glue thickly over a circle of stiff card and arrange pebbles on top.
✧ Collect some smooth beach pebbles and paint on them, for example a face, an animal, or an insect. When the paint is dry glaze them.
✧ Examine a piece of dry seaweed — it looks dead. Now put it in water. Watch it come to life! A chamois leather behaves in the same way.
✧ Read the poem 'Voices of Water' on page 74 and sing 'What's that Bobbing in the Sea?' on page 86.
✧ Make a 'Beside the Seaside' display (see page 61).

ISLANDS

Objective

Music — To respond to musical signals while playing a game of 'islands'.

Group size

The whole group.

What you need

Someone who can play the piano or if not available, a cassette player and tape of popular music — such as nursery rhymes or current 'pop' songs that the children like. Very large sheets of green 'activity' or sugar paper (or double sheet spread of a newspaper) to be used as islands. You will need one sheet of paper per three children.

Preparation

To make your islands look a bit more realistic cut the paper irregularly and round off the corners. You could draw one or two trees on them using a broad-tipped marker.

What to do

The children will have to listen carefully for when the music stops and starts. To give them listening practice while they are sitting still, ask them to clap once, each time the music stops or starts. Spread the 'islands' on the floor with plenty of space in between them. They are going to 'paddle' and 'swim' round these islands in the sea while the music is playing (avoiding stepping on the islands). Show them how to move their arms for breast stroke, crawl or doggy paddle.

When the music stops it means that there is a shark in the water that is trying to catch them. They should hop on to the nearest island as quickly as possible. They must not have even a foot in the water or the shark will get them! There is no need for anyone to be 'out' — just continue playing until everyone is tired.

Discussion

An island is a piece of land surrounded by water. Some islands used to be part of the mainland but the sea has 'cut' them off. Can the children think of ways of getting from one island to another without getting wet? Ferries can transport cars and lorries as well as people. Some islands are connected to the mainland by long bridges and tunnels.

Follow-up activities

✧ Look at a map of the world and find the islands. Compare them using the words: small, smaller, smallest; big, bigger, biggest.
✧ Give each child a copy of a simplified map of the British Isles and ask them to colour round the islands of Great Britain and Ireland using a blue crayon to represent the sea.
✧ Make two islands for the water tray using construction toys, then make a bridge which will connect them.
✧ Sing the song 'My Little Island' on page 87.

BOBBING UP AND DOWN

Objective

Design and Technology – To design and make a boat which will float.

Group size

Six children.

What you need

Teacup and saucer, cereal bowl, small glass jar, small tin, bits of wood, an assortment of the following: take-away food containers, blocks of polystyrene packing material, corks, dried out skins from half an orange or grapefruit, walnut shells; Blu-Tack, Plasticine, play dough, cocktail sticks, lolly sticks and straws for masts, paper, card or silver foil for sails, sticky tape, scissors, the water tray or a large washing up bowl with water.

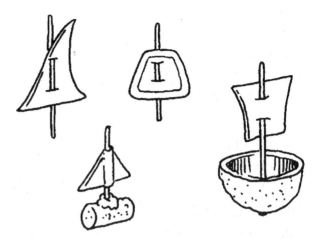

What to do

Let the children handle all the different materials and predict which they think will float. Ask them to choose one of the materials which they think they can use to make a sailing boat. They will need to decide what shape they want to cut from the card or foil to make the sail. Ask them to suggest ways in which they can attach the sail to the boat. When their boat is made let them see if it will float on water.

Discussion

Do they know why some of the boats sank? When some of the boats went to the bottom and sank it was because they were too heavy for the water to hold them up. Water can hold air up easily because air is lighter than water. Why do some boat shapes float better than others? The more air that can fit into the boat the better it will float. Did some of the boats topple over? Sometimes the sail is too tall and causes the boat to overbalance. What other types of boats can the children think of? (Rowing boat, raft, tug, canoe, yacht.)

Follow-up activities

✧ Try ways to make the boats move (push, blow, blow through a straw, disturb the water).
✧ Have a boat race with all the boats you've made.
✧ Blow up a balloon just a little and seal it. Try and push it under the water. What happens?
✧ Add a sunken boat to 'The Deep Blue Sea' display on page 60.
✧ Try floating a papier mâché food tray. How long before it sinks and why?
✧ Say 'Rub-a-dub-dub three men in a tub'.

SHIP AHOY!

Objective

Music – To sing a song and make the appropriate actions.

Group size

The whole group.

What you need

The song 'The big ship sails on the Alley, Alley O' which can be found in the book *Oranges and Lemons* compiled by Karen King (OUP).

What to do

Ask the children to help arrange their chairs side by side in rows and sit down – at least five in a row to make it effective. Show them how to 'link' arms as if they were a chain. Sing the song with the following actions:

• First verse – with linked arms all sway first to one side then to the other (leaning against each other).
• Second verse – un-link arms and point and shake their index finger, as if they were telling someone off while they sing: 'The captain said it will never never do'.
• Third verse – stand up and bend knees to the ground, going up and down. (Holding hands while bending makes this more difficult and more fun.)
• Fourth verse – sit down and keep nodding their heads up and down while they sing.

You could end off with a repeat of the first verse because the children love linking arms!

Discussion

A ship is a large sea-going boat. It has windows called *portholes* and rooms called *cabins*. What are ships used for? They can move people, cars, animals and goods called *cargo*. Sometimes people go for a holiday or cruise on a ship and visit lots of different countries. They walk across the *gangplank* (portable bridge) to get on and off the ship. If there is a fierce storm or water gets in through a large hole, ships will sink and become *shipwrecks*. They will also sink if too much cargo is loaded on them.

Follow-up activities

◇ Float a polystyrene food tray. Gradually add some weights – nails or marbles. How many will the tray hold before it sinks?
◇ Write a message in a bottle from someone who has been in a shipwreck.
◇ Find a picture of an old sailing ship; a galleon. Count how many sails it has and look at the differently shaped sails.

DROP ANCHOR

Objective

Geography – To make two 'boats' to demonstrate that ships need to anchor in shallow water to prevent them floating away.

Group size

Six children.

What you need

Water in the water tray, a handful of small pebbles, two soap measure-balls (they come with liquid clothes detergent), a skewer and Plasticine, a piece of string (approx 50cm), a weight such as a strong iron bolt.

Preparation

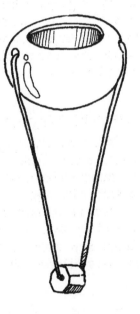

Take one measure-ball and make a hole in each side by pushing the skewer through the plastic rim using the Plasticine as a buffer. Thread the string through the two holes and tie the ends together. Secure the bolt to the string so that it will drop below the ball (see diagram). This is a boat with its anchor! The other ball is a boat without anchor and does not need any preparation.

What to do

The children can drop the pebbles in a pile at one end of the water tray, as if it were the seabed. Let them place both boats in the water so that one drops its anchor to catch in the pebbles. Ask them to make gentle and then more vigorous waves with their hands in the 'sea', but not so much that the boats become waterlogged! Ask them to note what happens to both the boats. Show the children how to blow across the boats as if it were very windy. Again, note what happens to the boats.

Discussion

Sea water is shallower along the coast. Natural harbours on the coast are sheltered from bad weather and stormy seas; they have narrow openings for ships and boats to come and go. Boats need to drop their anchor to stop floating away. Would a boat be able to anchor in the middle of the ocean? (Too deep.) Sometimes harbours need to be built – these are often called *docks*. What are these docks used for? (Ships to unload their cargos, ferries to pick up and put down their passengers.) Anchors are often not enough to hold a ship in place, what do the children think could be used to help? (Ropes tied to platforms, called *quays*.) Anchors used to be just heavy stones but nowadays they are made from iron and have sharp points called *flukes* which dig into the seabed.

Follow-up activities

✧ Give each child a copy of photocopiable page 90 to match the anchors to the ships by size.
✧ Trace around the coastline of a map of the British Isles with a finger and find the harbours of London, Glasgow and Liverpool.
✧ Dramatise the loading and unloading of people and cargo from a ship.
✧ Read the poem 'The Harbour Wall on page 68.
✧ Practice tying knots using thick string.
✧ Blow across the top of a bottle neck to make the sound of a ship's whistle coming from its funnel.

JONAH AND THE WHALE

Objective

Religious Education – To listen to a biblical story and make a picture of a whale.

Group size

Six children.

What you need

A story about Jonah and the Whale (see page 75), an outline of a whale for each child on a sheet of A4 sized paper, one new black bin liner, a pair of sharp scissors, three empty containers (for example, cottage cheese cartons), three pots of PVA glue, six glue spreaders, six blue crayons, some cotton wool (for water spray).

Preparation

Draw a whale outline and make a copy for each child. Cut up some of the bin bag into 1cm squares (approximately) and divide the squares into each of the three containers.

What to do

Read or tell the children the story of Jonah and the Whale. Give each child a whale outline and let them share a container of black squares and a glue pot, one between two. Ask the children to colour in the whale's eye with a blue crayon. Show them how to overlap the black squares and stick them all over the whale — including its tail. Warn them not to cover up the whale's eye. Let them glue some wispy bits of cotton wool above the whale to represent its spray. Finally ask them to fill in the sea using the blue crayon.

Discussion

Talk about the story of how a man could get inside a whale. A whale is the largest mammal we know that has ever lived. A whale can be three times bigger than the largest known dinosaur. It's tongue can be heavier than an elephant (for example, the Blue Whale). It looks like a fish but is different because it can't stay under the water all the time. Why does it keep coming up above the water? As it breathes out through blow-holes on the top of its head, water vapour hisses up into the air and looks like smoke. Some whales don't have teeth so when they want food they simply open their mouth very wide and trap lots of sea creatures in the hairy fringed ridges in their mouths.

Follow-up activities

✧ Say the tongue-twister: 'Why do wise whales watch white wheels wobble?'
✧ Make a whale out of clay or play dough. Don't forget the blow-holes!
✧ Put a black sock on you hand and pretend it's a whale. Move your whale on top of the table, under your chair, next to your other hand, into your pocket, above your head, behind your back.
✧ Look at the pictures of Jonah in the whale in the *Bible Story Book* by Georgie Adams (Orion).
✧ Say the poem 'Whale' from *The Book of a Thousand Poems* (Collins).

CHAPTER 3
FRESH WATER

Water is never very far from us. It collects in puddles, ponds and reservoirs;
streams trickle down from mountains and join rivers; canals provide routes
for holiday barges; swimming baths enable us to swim in safety.
This chapter looks at these forms of inland water.

RIBBONS OF WATER

Objective

Geography – To find out that water from streams always flows in a downwards direction and eventually joins rivers.

Group size

Six children.

What you need

Deep sand in the sand tray, water in a watering can with an end-cap (rose) with holes in it, a length of blue ribbon.

What to do

Ask the children to help you pile the sand to one end of the tray so that it looks like a hill with a gentle slope. Hold the watering can well above the 'hill' and sprinkle the water over the highest part as if it were rain. At first the water will disappear as it is soaked up by the sand but eventually it will form its own little streams and flow down towards the bottom of the 'hill'. Once the water has formed streams, continue to sprinkle more water which will make its way down the same channels. Notice what happens to the channel water at the bottom of the 'hill'.

Discussion

Ask the children where the first water drops disappeared to. When it rains the ground always soaks up some of the water and when it cannot soak up any more, the following water has to find somewhere else to go. It forms little streams that look like blue ribbons. When water flows down a hillside it often leaves a V shape in the ground as it carries the soil and stones. Was any of the sand moved with the water? Water always flows downhill but it does not always go in straight lines. What patterns did the water make in the sand? Streams meet each other like the channels in the sand tray, and then form rivers. These rivers are always moving downwards towards the sea. Streams run into rivers like side roads meet main roads or motorways.

Follow-up activities

✧ Practise writing V, the shape that the water makes as it flows down the hill, through the valley.
✧ Use a fork or comb to make patterns in the damp sand.
✧ Children can be streams running from different directions and meeting together at 'the river'.
✧ Read the poem 'The growing river' in the *Book of a Thousand Poems* (Collins).

WATERFALLS ARE BUBBLY

Objective

Art – To blow air bubbles into coloured water and make a picture.

Group size

Three children at a time.

What you need

Three glass bowls of approximately 15cm diameter, water, washing-up liquid, mixing fork, three colours of ready mixed or liquid paint, at least one straw and one piece of painting paper for each child, glasses of water and an empty bowl. Picture of a waterfall if possible.

Preparation

Half fill the three glass bowls with approximately one part liquid soap to two parts water. Add enough paint to make a strong colour and mix it in with the fork. Experiment to see if the mixture will bubble up above the rim of the bowl when blown through a straw.

What to do

Ensure the children know the difference between sucking and blowing. Ask each child to blow through a straw on to their hand and feel the air. Then get the children to suck and blow through a straw in clear water so that they realise the difference. Let them practise this for a while before they go on to blowing into a bowl of soapy coloured water. They should do this until it bubbles right up over the top. Place a piece of paper over the top of the bubbles, pressing down gently so that the bubbles leave an imprint when the paper is peeled off. Repeat the process with the other two colours. Use a glass of water and empty bowl for any child who still sucks instead of blows.

Discussion

What's inside bubbles? (Air.) Did the children notice how the bubbles stuck together, changed shape and kept bursting? When water is moved quickly it traps little bubbles of air which stick together and make it look frothy. Where have the children seen frothy water? The waves which break on the beach look frothy, so does fast running bath water. River water flowing over the sharp edge of rocks forms a waterfall. The falling water traps air in tiny bubbles and makes the water look like white foam.

Follow-up activities

✧ Use a rotary or balloon whisk to make water froth up.
✧ Shake a bottle of soda water and unscrew the top slowly (over a bowl). Hear the hiss and watch the 'fizz' spurt out.
✧ Fill a transparent polythene bottle with water nearly to the top. Tighten the lid and notice the bubble when you lay it on its side. Use this spirit level to test for flat surfaces.
✧ Make different shaped loops out of wire. Dip them into soapy water then blow through them. What shape are the bubbles? Blow again and try to catch the bubbles.
✧ Say the poems 'Bubbles' and 'The Waterfall' on pages 71 and 72.

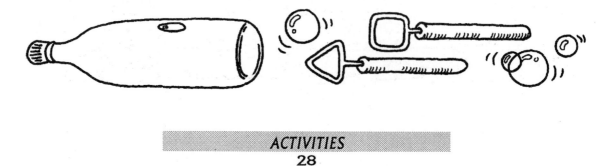

28

WATER

RIPPLES

Objective

Mathematics – To make a pattern by placing different sized circles in order.

Group size

Six children.

What you need

A deep, dark coloured washing-up bowl of water and a medicine dropper. For each child a paper plate of 15cm diameter and one paper circle of each of the following approximate sizes: 8cm, 7cm, 6cm, 5cm, two containers of PVA glue and one spreader. Some coloured felt-tipped pens or crayons.

Preparation

Cut all the circles to the diameters given above – a few extra ones might be useful. Sort the different sized circles on to the paper plates so that there is a set for each child – but not in size order.

What to do

Put the bowl of water on the floor and let the children stand round and wait for the water to be absolutely still. Use the medicine dropper to drop a single drop of water into the bowl and note what happens. Give each child their set of circles and show them how to sort them into size order across the table in front of them, starting with the biggest. When they have managed this ask them to stick the circles on top of each other so that all the edges can be seen. Let them colour each circle differently.

Discussion

What happened when the drop of water reached the water in the bowl? If a large still surface of water is disturbed in some way, little circular waves or ripples will form. These start off small in the middle and become bigger and bigger as they spread to the edges of the bowl, puddle, pond, lake or reservoir. Have any of the children ever thrown pebbles into the sea and seen the pattern that is made? If a duck swims across water it causes little waves but this time the ripples are V shaped.

Follow-up activities

✧ Blow on to the surface of the water with a straw and see what patterns appear. Can a 'hole' be blown down in the water?

✧ Wet some paper with a sponge and water. Drop a blob of paint on to it and watch how the colour spreads out towards the edge.

✧ Write a V in the middle of a page and write another V outside it using a different coloured crayon. Keep drawing more and more bigger V's until the page is full.

✧ Look at some raspberry ripple ice-ream. Make some similar ripples in plain yoghurt by gently stirring in some blackcurrant juice.

ROUND AND ROUND A WATERMILL

Objective

Music — To sing and play a musical water action game to gain understanding of the power of water.

Group size

The whole group.

What you need

A commercial toy water-wheel, watering can or large jug of cold water, a water tray or a large container to stand the water-wheel in, picture of a water-mill if possible.

What to do

Let the children handle the water-wheel and see what they have to do to make it turn round (push, pull, press). Place the wheel in the water trough and pour water on to it from above. Note what happens to the wheel. Practise singing the following words to the tune of 'Ring-a-ring o' roses':

> Round and round the wheel goes
> As the river water flows,
> Tip-up, tip-up!
> It all falls down.

When the children know the words ask them to form a circle holding hands. If necessary form two smaller circles rather than one big one — circles with more than ten children tend to disintegrate! Decide which way round you are going to turn and proceed to dance round singing the song. When you get to 'Tip-up, tip-up!' they should bend from their waists as if they were bowing and then finally — all fall down. When choosing the direction in which to circle it may be a good time to introduce the concept of left and right, or to point out the direction of clock numbering.

Discussion

Fast flowing or falling water can be powerful enough to move things. Have the children noticed their bath toys moving about in the water while the bath fills up? Many years ago wheat was made into flour by the grains being crushed between two huge round flat pieces of stone. Can the children guess what turned the mill-stones round? They were too big and heavy to be moved by hand and so were often moved by a water-wheel. Flour mills used to be built next to rivers where there was a constant flow of water which could be used to turn the water-wheel.

Follow-up activities

✧ Crush some wholewheat grains (from a healthfood shop) in a pestle and mortar, to produce flour.

✧ Position the point of a thick pencil in the middle of a page and draw round and round in the same direction to form a spiral.

✧ If there is a hose pipe available pinch the end of it to make a strong jet of water and see how it can move dirt and leaves off a path.

MY HOUSEBOAT

Objective

Design and Technology — To design and make furniture for a toy canal houseboat.

Group size

Eight children.

What you need

Construction kits, two shoeboxes of the same size, an assortment of the following: match-boxes, egg boxes and other small boxes, pieces of polystyrene, small containers such as plastic drink and washing-up liquid bottles, camera, film canisters, container lids, empty cotton reels, corks, ice-lolly sticks, cocktail sticks, used matchsticks, spills, drinking straws and Artstraws, cardboard tubes and pieces of plain and corrugated cardboard, scissors, sharp craft knife (for adults only), Plasticine, PVA adhesive, sticky tape, masking tape, rubber bands, paper-clips, paper fasteners, scraps of material and carpet. Ask in advance and the children will enjoy collecting and bringing in many of these items from home.

Preparation

Use two shoeboxes stuck together with a V shape at one end to form one long narrow boat. The diagram below shows what the end result should look like.

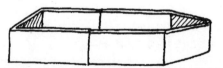

2 shoeboxes stuck together for a narrowboat

What to do

Show the children the narrow boat and ask them what type of furniture they would need if this was to be a home. From the collection of materials you have gathered ask them to choose things to make a piece of furniture to go into the houseboat. They will need to plan for a limited space. If they get stuck suggest some of the ideas from the illustrations on this page.

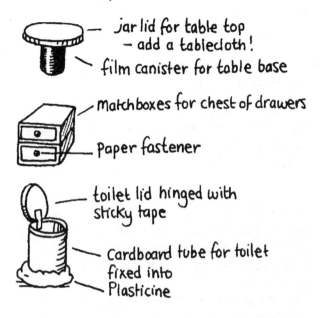

polystyrene food tray with fabric covers and pillows for double bed.

jar lid for table top — add a tablecloth!

film canister for table base

matchboxes for chest of drawers

paper fastener

toilet lid hinged with sticky tape

cardboard tube for toilet fixed into Plasticine

Discussion

Canals are man-made waterways which were built a long time ago. They can connect rivers to each other. In the past, narrow flat-bottomed boats called barges or narrow boats, were pulled (towed) by horses who walked along the side of the canal on the tow-path. The barges used to take goods to different places around the country. What do we use now? (Roads, railways.) These days some narrow boats are used as holiday homes. Can the children think of other holiday homes which move and where space is limited? (Caravans.)

Follow-up activities

✧ Arrange the furniture in the cardboard narrow boat and let the dolls-house people 'live' in it.
✧ Make a narrow boat with an empty date box and see if it will float.
✧ Let the children improvise a houseboat using the furniture in the room. When they play in such a confined space they may realise what it would be like to live on a houseboat.
✧ Say the poem 'A Good Play' in *A Child's Garden of Verses* by Robert Louis Stevenson (Wordsworth).

MOSES IS HIDING

Objective

Religious Education – To reinforce the idea that babies are still as precious as when Moses was hidden among the bulrushes; to weave a basket.

Group size

The whole group for the story, then a group per basket of four to six children.

What you need

A copy of the story of Moses in the Bulrushes (*The Lion Storyteller Bible*), two wire hanging baskets (or a freezer or laundry basket), strips of fabric, paper, thick wool and string in colours of greens, browns and yellows, a pair of children's scissors each, one pair of sharp scissors (for adults), something woven from natural rush or straw such as a shopping bag or table mat.

Preparation

Cut the fabric into long strips approximately 2.5cm wide by 1 metre long. These can be used by the children as a guide for cutting similar sized strips of paper and pieces of wool.

What to do

Read the story of Moses in the Bulrushes and talk about how important it was to make a basket to protect the baby Moses. Show the children the woven basket or mat and talk about weaving. Put the children into two groups (one group per basket) and ask an adult supervisor to help. Let the children cut strips of paper and wool and show them how to weave the basket with these and the strips of fabric. Give each child a turn at weaving. Try to fill in all the gaps. Use the materials and colours at random to give the impression of a shaded basket. The children could be decorating their strips of paper while others weave. You could use long leaves and grasses to be more realistic but these may be too sharp for children.

Discussion

Around the edges of ponds, rivers and lakes, the ground is often very wet. It feels spongy and soft when you walk on it. This marshy, wetland area is perfect for tall grass reeds to grow. Reeds are especially good for weaving baskets. Bulrushes are tall reeds which grow so thickly that they make a good hiding place for birds' nests. The hollow stems of the reeds provide shelter for insects. Have the children ever seen a baby's carry-cot woven from reeds? What else is made from grasses? (Thatched roofs, chair seats, waste-paper baskets.)

Follow-up activities

✧ Settle a doll into the woven basket, hide it and play a game of hunt the Moses basket.
✧ Make your own patch of wetland by thoroughly soaking an area of grass. Test how it feels when you stand on it.
✧ Straw is dried grass stalks. Use some hollow pieces to blow bubbles into water. This could be linked to 'Waterfalls are bubbly' on page 28.
✧ Say the poem 'All Along the Backwater' and the tongue-twister 'Moses supposes his toeses' from *Knock at the Door* by Jan Betts (Ward Lock).

HELLO ME!

Objective

Mathematics – To look down into water and see that it acts like a mirror and will reflect images.

Group size

Six children.

What you need

A dark-coloured washing-up bowl (if this is not available, line the bowl with a piece of brown or black paper), large jug of water, torch.

What to do

Place the empty washing-up bowl on the floor and ask the children to stand round and look down into it. What can they see? Fill the bowl with water, wait until the water settles and ask the children what they can see now. Shine the torch on the water and ask the children to look at the ceiling. Disturb the water very slightly and note what happens to the reflection of the torchlight on the ceiling.

Discussion

Could the children see themselves in the empty bowl? What about when the water had settled in it? What did the torchlight on the ceiling look like while the water was moving? Where can reflections be seen outside? Puddles and ponds have still water which reflects the scenes around them, making them look as if they are upside down! Ponds are holes or dips in the ground filled with water. They can be natural or man-made. Ponds always have some form of life, even if it is only green slimy algae (water-plants) on the surface. Can the children name any other pond life? (Water lilies, frogs, tadpoles, dragonflies, pond skaters, snails, water boatmen, ducks, moorhens.) Children should never stand near the edge of a pond without adult supervision.

Follow-up activities

✧ Give each child a copy of photocopiable page 91. Let them place a mirror along the dotted edge of each shape and then draw the reflections on to their sheet.

✧ Look at your reflection on different shiny objects such as both sides of a spoon, a biscuit tin lid, a magnified cosmetic mirror, a car hub-cap. Do you look like you?

✧ Ask a dentist for a mouth mirror and show the children how the dentist looks at their teeth. (Dip the mirror into a sterilising liquid between mouths.)

✧ Look through a kaleidoscope and make your own. Fix two mirrors in Plasticine so that they face each other with a toy in between them. How many toys can you can see in one of the mirrors?

✧ Say the poem 'Park Pond' on page 68 and sing the song 'Hello me' on page 85.

✧ Read the poems 'The Mirror' in *When We Were Very Young* (Methuen) and 'Upside Down World' in *The Book of a Thousand Poems* (Collins).

LEISURE TIME

Objective

Physical Education — To move and play in ways which are lots of fun when in the water.

Group size

The whole group.

What you need

One large light beach ball, preferably made of inflatable plastic, armbands (ask the children to bring their own if they have them), the water tray.

What to do

Let the children examine the armbands and test them on the water before and after they are inflated. Allow them to try them on. Explain their purpose and that providing the children are wearing them and are supervised by an adult, it is quite safe to play some games in the swimming baths. Moving in water is much slower and more difficult than moving out of water. Show the children how to move round the room in a 'dragging' fashion as if the water was holding them back. Ask them to take a deep breath, put their heads 'under the water' and see how long before they have to come up for air. (Do not allow this to become a competition!) Let them form a circle (around the edge of the swimming pool) and when you give the signal they can all jump in (being careful not to bump into others). Now it's time to play water ball. The children take it in turns to throw and catch. They must remember that if the ball is dropped, they need to wade through the water to pick it up again.

Discussion

Water can be very dangerous and children must never go near water without an adult. Even the changing rooms and water's edge at a leisure centre can be dangerous and slippery so the children should move about very carefully. Do they know the difference between shallow and deep water? Is it better to open or close your fingers when you are swimming? What kind of leisure activities can people do in and on the water? (Water skiing, sailing, rowing, surfing, fishing, aerobics.)

Follow-up activities

✧ Practise going down the slide steps (backwards) as one would getting into a swimming bath.
✧ Paint a picture which shows that deep water is darker in colour than shallow water.
✧ Sit behind each other on the floor and see if you can all row in time — first with the left arm and then with the right arm.
✧ Examine a polystyrene float. Pretend that a book is a float and hold onto it as you lie on your tummy on the floor kicking your legs.
✧ Read the story 'Indoor Sports" on page 76.

CHAPTER 4
WATER AT HOME

We couldn't manage our lives without water. We use it everyday
in our homes for washing ourselves, our clothes and cleaning our houses.
How could we cook and wash up if we didn't have water?
Water even tells us where the puncture is in a car tyre.

EUREKA!

Objective

History – To find out that people in the past made discoveries about water and to test out a fable.

Group size

Six children.

What you need

The fable 'The Crow and the Pitcher' *Aesop's Fables*, retold by Jacqueline Morley (Macdonald), tall drinking glass, breakfast bowl, indelible black marker pen, clean pebbles of approximately 2cm diameter (from garden centres or builders' merchants), jug of cold water.

What to do

Read or tell the children the story of 'The Crow and the Pitcher'. Tell them the pitcher is a large narrow-necked jug for storing water and is usually made of earthenware. It is not a picture on the wall! Explain that you are all going to try the crow's trick. Fill the drinking glass three-quarters with water, mark the level with a line all the way round the glass and place it in the breakfast bowl. Let the children take it in turns to add one pebble at a time into the glass of water. Ask them to predict what will happen. When the water overflows into the dish say 'Eureka!'

Discussion

A long time ago a Greek man called Archimedes went to have a bath and as he sat down in the water he noticed that the level rose up. He was so pleased to make this discovery that he jumped out of his bath and ran around shouting Eureka, eureka! which means 'I have found it'. The crow in the story had discovered Archimedes', idea but instead of shouting out 'Eureka!' what did he do? (Have a drink.) What happens to the water when the children get into their bath? What happens if there are two children in the bath at once?

Follow-up activities

✧ Half fill a dolls' bath with water, mark the level, add some heavy dolls and mark the new level. Make the level rise and fall – add and subtract the dolls.
✧ Play hunt the thimble and shout 'Eureka!' when you have found it.
✧ Find Greece on a map of the world.
✧ Count some pebbles to 'Tinker, Tailor, Soldier, Sailor' from *The Oxford Nursery Rhyme Book*.
✧ Read the story *Mr Archimedes' Bath* by Pamela Allen (Puffin).

LOTS OF SHAPES

* *

Objective

Mathematics – To be aware that water changes its shape without changing its amount.

Group size

Six children.

What you need

A thin polythene bag not less than 22cm wide and 35cm long (under the supervision of an adult), a rubber band, 400g of cold water in a jug, a shallow washing-up bowl, a 500g circular plastic (cottage cheese) container, a 500g square plastic food container, an empty half litre glass measuring jug, one litre clear plastic drink bottle (for example, soda water), tea towel.

Preparation

Pour 400g of water into the polythene bag. Squeeze the air out of it before securing it with the rubber band just below the top. Cut the top part off the plastic bottle. Hide the measuring jug, plastic bottle, circular and square containers under the tea towel.

What to do

Ask the children: 'Can I make this water (in the bag) into a square shape?' Produce the square container from under the tea towel and place it into the shallow washing-up bowl (in case of spills!). Manoeuvre the bag of water so that the bottom corners are empty. Introduce these corners first into the container and let the rest of the bag of water follow. It should fit comfortably with the rubber band uppermost. Now ask: 'Can I make this water into the shape of a bottle?' Repeat the process with the other two containers. It's magic!

Discussion

Water does not have its own shape but takes the shape of anything that it is put into. Do the children think that any of the containers had more water in than the others? Was any water added? What other shapes can water take – teapots, vases, buckets, baths, paddling pools, puddles, ponds? What else can be poured into different shapes – sand, salt and sugar? Explain the difference between full and empty. Full means you can't get any more in and empty means you can't get any more out!

Follow-up activities

✧ Give each child the same amount of water in a glass and let them choose from an assortment of different containers which shape they want to change their water into. They may need to pour it through a funnel.
✧ Describe an assortment of bottles and other containers as: wide, narrow, flat, round, square, short, tall, empty, full, half full.
✧ Say the poem 'The shape of water' on page 73.
✧ Watch sand change shape in an egg-timer.
✧ Estimate how many cupfuls of water are needed to fill a jug, a bowl, a bucket. Fill them and check your estimate.

SHADY PAINTS

Objective

Art – To paint stripes using liquid paint which has been gradually diluted with water.

Group size

Two children at a time.

What you need

A paint pot, a dry broad paint brush (approximately 1.5cm wide) and a piece of white paper (A4) for each child, a small jug of cold water and a teaspoon, strong coloured liquid paints.

What to do

Give each child a piece of white paper and explain that they are going to paint some stripes. Let them choose a colour and see you put a generous blob of liquid paint into their paint pot. Ask them to paint a stripe down the left hand side of the paper using the dry brush. They may need to dip in a couple of times to get an even thick deep stripe. Next let each child add one teaspoonful of water into their paint pot and mix it in with the brush, before painting another stripe next to the first one. Then the children can mix in another teaspoonful of water and paint the third stripe alongside the other two. They should continue adding a teaspoonful of water before painting another stripe, until the page is full of stripes. Notice the differences between the stripes.

Discussion

When water is added to most liquids (not oils) it dilutes them. This means they become weaker in strength and look lighter in colour. What has happened to their painted stripes? (They have gone paler and paler.) Which drinks need to be diluted? (Orange squash, blackcurrant juice, Bovril.) When a can of concentrated soup is diluted you get double the amount of soup! Liquid plant food is far too strong to give to plants straight from the bottle – how can it be weakened?

Follow-up activities

✧ Count how many shades of each colour there are on a decorator's shade card.
✧ Pour some concentrated juice into a glass and fill it with ice cubes. When the cubes have melted what has happened to the juice?

concentrated drink with ice cubes   ice has melted, diluting the concentrated drink

✧ Add some drops of liquid food colouring to a glass of water and watch how the colour is weakened as it drifts in the water.
✧ Soak a brand new yellow duster in very hot water over night. Next day note the colour of the water. When the duster is dry compare its colour to another new duster.

SOAKING PEAS

Objective

Mathematics — To weigh peas before and after they have been soaked in water.

Group size

Six children.

What you need

A 500g packet of dried marrowfat peas (not frozen), food scales, straining spoon, a litre glass bowl, jug of cold water, white card, a pen.

What to do

Point out that the scales are registering zero. Ask each child in turn to take a handful of peas, place them on the scales and watch what happens to the number dial. Note how the peas feel and smell and whether they make a noise as they are put on to the scales. Have a turn yourself to ensure that the scales register an easily recognisable number! Ask an able child to write the dry weight of all the peas on the card. Another child can tip the peas into the glass bowl and cover them with water to come just below the rim of the bowl. Leave the peas to soak for 24 hours. Next day, check that the scales register zero before lifting the soaked peas on to the scales using the straining spoon. Compare the weight and texture of the soaked and dry peas. Ensure that nobody eats any of the peas.

dried peas just put into water.

after 24 hours have swollen with water.

Discussion

How did the dry peas feel and smell? What noise did they make when they were weighed? (Rattled, clattered.) How do the soaked peas feel (softer) and smell? Do they make a noise when they are put on the scales? Compare the size of a dried pea to that of a soaked pea. What has made the peas change? Water changes things and when some foods are covered with water, they suck it up (absorb it).

Follow-up activities

✦ Arrange 20 dried peas in a row next to each other. Make a similar row underneath of 20 soaked peas. Compare the length of the row.

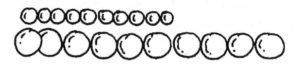

✦ Pour some boiling water on to a packet of dried soup. See and smell what happens. (Make sure the children don't taste without your permission.)
✦ Use some dried peas for pretend cooking in the home corner.
✦ Sing 'Here comes Mrs Macaroni' from *The Funny Family* (Ward Lock Educational).
✦ Say the action rhyme 'Five fat peas' from *Round and Round the Garden* by Sarah Williams (OUP).
✦ Read the story 'The Princess and the Pea' *Fairy Tale* series (Michael O'Mara Books).

VEGETABLE SOUP

Objective

Design and Technology — To select, prepare and cook vegetables to make a soup.

Group size

Four children at a time.

What you need

A bowl of cold water, food scales, four pairs of children's scissors, two chopping knives, two chopping boards, potato peeler, grater, large pan with a lid, boiling ring, two medium sized carrots, one large potato, two sticks of celery, one leek, two tomatoes, two cabbage leaves, 30g red lentils, 30g alphabet vermicelli, two vegetable stock cubes, one teaspoonful of salt and sugar, one litre of cold water, cups for everyone.

What to do

The children should wash their hands before handling and examining the raw vegetables. Ask them to wash the cabbage leaves, leeks, celery and tomatoes and use the peeler for the potato and carrots. They will need to decide which tools will be best to prepare the other vegetables. The carrots can be grated, the leeks and celery cut into thin strips with the knife and then cut with scissors, the potato and tomatoes chopped with the knives. Closely supervise the use of the grater, peeler and knives. This is a good opportunity for the children to learn how to use them. Let the children put the chopped vegetables into the pan and add the lentils, vermicelli, crumbled stock cubes, salt, sugar and water. Bring the pan to the boil then reduce the heat to simmering for about an hour. Taste it and add more seasonings or water if necessary.

Smell and look at the soup before, during and after the cooking process. Sit down and enjoy a cup of soup together.

Discussion

When water is used to cook vegetables, it softens them and blends their flavours to make soups and stews. Could the children recognise the vegetable pieces when the soup was cooked? Where had the lentils gone and what had happened to the vermicelli? What other foods need water before they can be eaten? (Boiled eggs, jellies, boiled rice.)

Follow-up activities

✧ Use the alphabet letters from some dry vermicelli to make your name.
✧ Cut a stick of celery into a long fringe and cross cut a radish. Leave them overnight in a bowl of cold water and the next day see how the celery curls and the radish makes a rose shape.
✧ Chant 'Chop chop choppity chop' from *This Little Puffin*, Elizabeth Matterson (Puffin).
✧ Thump your fists on top of each other and say
   *1 potato 2 potatoes 3 potatoes 4,
   5 potatoes 6 potatoes 7 potatoes more!*
✧ Read the story 'The Soup Stone' from *Six Folk Tales* adapted by Sheila Lane and Marion Kemp.

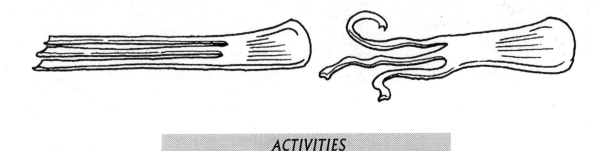

THE WAY WE WASH

Objective

Music – To mime the actions of washing ourselves to a song.

Group size

The whole group.

What you need

A bath sponge, flannel, loofah, back brush, bar of soap, an empty shampoo bottle, toothbrush and tube of toothpaste, towel.

What to do

Hold up the sponge and ask the children what it's for. Ask them to show you the actions they would make with it when washing. You may like to refine the action slightly for the children to copy! Repeat the process holding up each of the items in turn. Pretend to pour shampoo on to you hair and to put toothpaste on to the toothbrush. When you are satisfied that the children are familiar with the actions, form a ring with them. Explain that you are going to hold up each article in turn and they are to make the appropriate action while they sing these words to the tune of the Mulberry Bush:

> This is the way we sponge our tummies,
> sponge our tummies,
> sponge our tummies,
> This is the way we sponge our tummies,
> When it's time for bed.

Continue, substituting with:
✧ brush our backs,
✧ clean our teeth,
✧ flannel our faces,
✧ shampoo our hair,
✧ dry ourselves,
✧ loofah our legs,
✧ soap our hands.

Discussion

Apart from the articles which you have held up, what is the single most important thing that is needed to be able to wash yourself (clean water)? Is it important that people should be clean all the time? When doesn't it matter if you're not clean? (Doing a messy job, when you're playing and having fun.) When is it very important to be clean? (After going to the toilet, before handling food, when touching babies and sick people, on special social occasions like parties and Christmas.)

Follow-up activities

✧ Make a line of all the children who take baths and another line of those who take showers. Which line is longer; which is the most popular way to get clean? Can they suggest why?
✧ Put the loofah, flannel and sponge into a bowl of water. Guess which will hold the most water. Squeeze each one out into a separate glass bowl and see if your guess was right.
✧ Try washing hands with a soapless washing cream. Does it clean your hands properly?
✧ Make a display of all the things which are needed at bathtime – don't forget the bath toys!
✧ Say the poem 'Bathtime' on page 70.
✧ Sing 'Sam, Sam, the mucky old man' from *The Funny Family* (Ward Lock).
✧ Say the poem 'Before Tea' from *When We Were Very Young* by A. A Milne (Methuen).

WASHDAY

* *

Objective

History — To be aware that methods of washing clothes have changed since the past.

Group size

The whole group.

What you need

An outline of a washing machine (see photocopiable page 92) and a pair of scissors for each child, a coloured backing sheet (size A4), a craft knife, glue pots and spreaders, plenty of clothes magazines (from babies' and children's shops), a pile of clothes for sorting (dolls' and dressing-up clothes). If possible, have a display of some old washing equipment such as a corrugated washboard, wooden dolly or flat iron — alternatively use pictures of them (found in *The National Trust book of Forgotten Household Crafts* [Dorling Kindersley]).

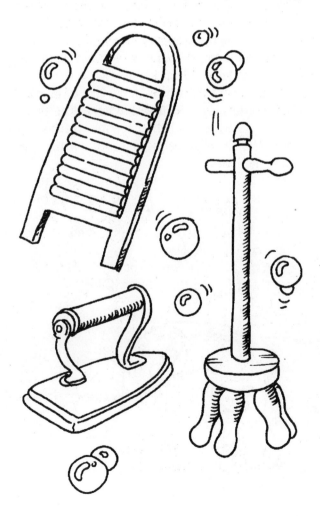

Preparation

Only do this if you feel the children are not able to, otherwise they can do it themselves. Cut round the dotted lines of the washing machine doors taking care not to cut through the hinges.

What to do

Help the children to sort the 'washing' into two piles — one of whites and one of coloureds. Ask them to cut out pictures of clothes from magazines and stick them overlapping (as they would be in a washing machine) in the middle of the coloured backing paper. As with the real clothes, they must make sure that no whites get mixed up with the coloureds. They will need to cut off any heads, arms and legs because these don't get washed in a washing machine! Finally stick the washing machine outline on to the backing paper ensuring that the door is wide open and the washing can be seen.

Discussion

Why do we sort clothes before washing them in a machine? (They need different temperatures, colours run.) Years ago before washing machines were invented, all dirty clothes, sheets and towels had to be washed separately by hand. Sometimes the clothes were rubbed hard on to a corrugated washboard to help loosen the dirt, or they were moved in a wash-tub by a dolly peg or washing bat. There were no spin driers so clothes had to be wrung out by hand or put through a mangle. Clothes were made either of wool or of cotton and became very creased when washed. If there were a lot of children in the family the washing and ironing could take all day.

Follow-up activities

✧ Spin round first clockwise then anti-clockwise like the drum on a washing machine.
✧ Say the action poem 'Washday' on page 69 and sing the song 'Washday' on page 82.
✧ Practice in pairs folding dolls sheets — match corner to corner, fold in half and then in half again.
✧ Sort and match a pile of socks into pairs — are there any left over or 'odd' ones?
✧ Sing 'O can you wash your father's shirt' from *The Funny Family* (Ward Lock).
✧ Say the poem 'I went to visit a friend one day' from *This Little Puffin*.

CRYING PUPPETS

Objective

Design and Technology – To make some finger puppets that cry to discover that water will get through any hole.

Group size

Two children at a time.

What you need

Paper, pencil and a disposable polythene, PVC or latex household glove for each child (bought in packs from a chemist or supermarket). A collection of different coloured permanent marker pens with fine and bullet points and including a yellow highlighter pen. A dressmaking pin, jug of cold water, an empty washing-up bowl.

What to do

Explain to the children that they are going to make finger puppets. First they should choose and practise drawing their characters on paper. Next, place a glove in front of each child (see diagram) and ask them to draw their five puppets on to the fingertips of the glove, choosing different coloured pens. Help them open up each finger as they put the finished glove on and curve their hand round to see their puppets. Ask each child which of their puppets are going to cry. Take off the glove and slip a thick pen down the appropriate glove fingers.

The children can use the pin to prick holes in the puppets' eyes. Hold the glove open over the washing-up bowl, pour some water into each finger and see which puppets they have chosen to cry! You may need to make the holes a little bigger.

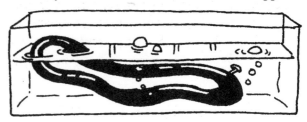

Discussion

A puncture is a small hole in something rubber or plastic. Can the children think of anything which they have seen that has been punctured? (A bicycle tyre, a football.) What does a football or car tyre look like when it has a hole in it? (It loses its shape and can be flattened.) When something with a hole in it is put into water, bubbles show where the hole is. This is because the water pushes air out as it finds its way through looking for more space.

Follow-up activities

◇ Hold a punctured bike tyre or hot water bottle (with lid on) under water in a bowl. Spot the bubbles as the water finds the hole.
◇ Make some holes in the upper half of a plastic drink bottle. Slowly fill it with water. Note that it only starts to leak when the water reaches the holes. Watch what happens to the water level below the holes.
◇ Fill a glass jar with pebbles. Pour some water in and watch as it finds its way round every stone filling all the spaces.
◇ Sing 'There's a hole in my bucket' from *Appusskidu* (A&C Black).
◇ Say the action rhyme 'Tommy Thumb' from *Round and Round the Garden* (OUP).

CHAPTER 5
LIVING THINGS NEED WATER

Some animals live in water and others feed from it, but all living things need water to survive. If countries are short of water they have to find ways of saving it. In this chapter the children will see the importance of keeping water clean enough to live in, to feed from and to drink.

FLIPPERS AND FLAPPERS

Objective

English – To practise letter recognition and discover how some birds have adapted to water.

Group size

The whole group.

What you need

Photocopiable page 93 for each child, pictures or photos of the following birds: duck, heron, penguin, swan (ensure that these pictures clearly show the parts of the birds mentioned below – or enlarge the photocopiable sheet), a piece of card (A3), a marker pen, pencils.

Preparation

Using the marker pen, write the lower case letters of the alphabet clearly and boldly onto the card, with spaces in between each letter.

What to do

Show the children the picture of the duck and ask who knows what kind of feet it has. Ask a child to come up to the alphabet card, point to the letter which 'webbed' begins with and draw a circle round it. Hold up the penguin picture, ask who knows what its 'arms' are called. Ask the child to circle the letter that 'flippers' begins with. Repeat the procedure with the heron's 'bill' and the swan's 'long neck'. Give each child a copy of photocopiable sheet 93 and ask them to write (in the box provided) the initial letter of the name of each bird in the pictures. They can then complete the unfinished pictures.

Discussion

Many birds live and feed in water. They are made (adapted) in different ways to make this easier for them. Why do ducks have webbed feet? (To prevent them slipping and sinking into the mud, and to help them swim.) Why do herons have dagger-like bills? (To spear their food.) They stand very still on their long legs in the water, waiting for fish to swim by. Why do penguins have flippers? (To help them swim very fast.) Penguins are birds without wings and can't fly. Why do swans have such long necks? (So that they can reach deep down into the water to find their food.)

Follow-up activities

✧ Ask the older children to overwrite the whole of the birds' names and then copy them underneath.
✧ Say the poem 'Mrs Indiarubber duck' by D. Carter in *The Book of a Thousand Poems* (Collins).
✧ Name other birds and say what letter of the alphabet they begin with.
✧ How would the children like to be adapted and for what purpose?

LITTLE MISS MUFFET

Objective

Science — To experiment and discover that many foods contain a lot of water.

Group size

Six children.

What you need

A half litre jug of full cream milk, half a fresh lemon, a litre size glass bowl, two drinking glasses, two teaspoons, lemon squeezer, small sieve, clean nappy liner or a coffee filter cone, piece of labelling card, yellow crayon.

What to do

Pour the milk into each glass (three-quarters full). Stir the glasses of milk with the teaspoons to see they are lump free. Leave the teaspoon in the glasses. Squeeze the juice from the lemon using the squeezer. Let those children who wish to, dip a clean finger into the lemon juice and taste it, then pour it into one of the glasses of milk. Ask a child to draw the picture of a lemon on the labelling card and place it next to the glass containing the lemon juice. Put both glasses of milk together in a warm place where you can see them. After five minutes stir the milk very gently and see what is left on the spoons. Line the sieve with filter paper, rest it in the glass bowl and after one hour pour the glass of 'lemon' milk through. When it has stopped dripping see what is left in the sieve and what is left in the bowl. Compare it to the other glass of milk.

Discussion

At first when the milk was stirred were there any 'threads' or lumps? What happened to the milk with the lemon juice after five minutes? (It went lumpy, thick, heavy.) When this lumpy milk was poured through the sieve did the children notice that the curds would not go through? What could get through the sieve? (The watery whey.) This shows that milk is more than three-quarters water. Had anything happened to the other glass of milk? Lemon juice is an acid which can separate milk into curds and whey. Cheese is made by separating milk. There is water in all living things including us! More than half of our bodies are made of water.

Follow-up activities

◇ Say the nursery rhyme 'Little Miss Muffet sat on her Tuffet'.
◇ Squeeze some oranges and drink the watery liquid they make.
◇ Write your name on paper using a paint brush and lemon juice. As it dries your name will become invisible. Hold the paper over a warm lamp bulb and see your name re-appear.
◇ Mash or pulp some strawberries, tomatoes or cucumbers, and see how much water comes out.
◇ Play a game of 'Oranges and Lemons'.

SANDY HANDS

Objective

English – To be aware that deserts are places which have very little rain and to practise handwriting skills using 'desert' sand.

Group size

Six children.

What you need

Two containers big enough to take an A4 sized piece of paper (equipment trays or new plastic cat litter trays), dry silver sand to cover the bottom of one container to a depth of 3cm, six pieces of paper (A4 size), glue sticks – if possible one for each child, an A3 sized piece of card, marker pen.

Preparation

Draw out the eight writing patterns on to the card [see below].

What to do

Show the children the card of writing patterns. To help maintain the rhythm of a writing pattern, chant as you write them. For example:

a dip 'nd a dip 'nd a dip

zig zag zig zag zig zag

dash dash dash dash dash

criss cross criss cross criss cross

a hump 'nd a hump 'nd a hump

dot dot dot dot dot

round 'nd round 'nd round 'nd round

Let the children take turns to practise their writing patterns in the sand with their forefinger. Shake the tray in between each pattern to level the surface. Now the children can 'write' the patterns on paper using the glue sticks. Place the paper in the empty tray and sprinkle sand on top. It will stick to the glue and 'show up' the writing patterns. Tip any excess sand back into the sand tray before the next child's turn.

Discussion

Sandy deserts are areas which have hardly any rain and not many plants and animals can stay alive there. Cactus type plants grow because they store water in their fleshy stalks. Camels can travel for long periods of time across the desert because their humps of fat are used for food and they can store water in their stomachs. They have large padded feet to walk across the soft sand and they can shut their nostrils against sandstorms. Some deserts have a stretch of water called an oasis where palm trees and vegetables will grow. The water at an oasis comes from under the ground.

conifer branch

camel

sand in tray   foil

Follow-up activities

◇ Make a pretend oasis. Line a polystyrene food tray with silver foil and pour sand over it. Push the sand away from the middle to show the 'water'. Add small pieces of conifer for palm trees and some plastic camels.
◇ Look at a map of North Africa and find the Sahara desert.
◇ Write your names on paper with glue and sand. Mix up the names and then see if you can 'feel' whose name it is with your eyes shut.
◇ Read the poem 'Camel' by William Jay Smith in *The Young Puffin Book of Verse*, compiled by Barbara Ireson (Puffin).

THIRSTY PEOPLE

Objective

Geography – To find out where water is collected (and stored) in preparation for a rain shortage; and to make a 'well'.

Group size

Six children.

What you need

Two straight-backed adult's chairs (with a slot in the back if possible), a long handled sweeping brush, 100cm length of thick string, a child's bucket, an adult's large bucket half filled with water, plenty of newspaper.

What to do

Place the chairs half a metre apart with their backs to each other. Push the handle of the brush through the gaps in the backs of the chairs or rest it across the top of the two chair-backs.

Tie one end of the string to the small bucket and the other end to the middle of the brush handle. Let two children stand at either end of the brush and 'wind' it so that the string coils and the small bucket lifts up towards the brush handle. Spread several layers of newspaper onto the floor between the chairs and put the large bucket of water on top, positioning it underneath the small bucket. Ask the children to turn the 'handle' and lower their small bucket into the bucket of water below. Fill the small bucket with water from the big bucket (you may need to help). Lastly ask the children to wind up their full bucket of water out of the 'well'.

Discussion

Some countries do not have rain very often therefore when it rains every bit of water has to be saved for times of drought. Water found under the ground lasts longer than that on the surface, because the sun cannot dry it up. How do people get the water out of the ground? (They need to build (sink) a well which will go deep into the ground to reach the water.) Drawing water up out of the ground can be very heavy work so sometimes oxen are used to wind up the buckets. People need to drink nearly 2.5 litres of water every day. In some countries where there is a shortage of water, it is sold by the cupful on the street. They buy a drink of water just like we buy ice lollies! In some places water comes out of the ground by itself forming natural springs.

Follow-up activities

✧ Pretend that the well you have made is a 'wishing well'. Aim a coin (or substitute) into the large bucket of water and make a wish.
✧ Sing the nursery rhyme 'Ding, dong, bell, Pussy's in the well'.
✧ Make a collection of different kinds of drinks which are made with water.
✧ Build a well using construction toys.

CATCH A FISH ALIVE

Objective

Mathematics – To practise counting and subtracting while playing a simple fish game.

Group size

A small group – not more than six.

What you need

A copy of photocopiable page 94, a piece of card [A3], enough thick coloured paper for approximately fifty fish, a container for the fish, scissors, dice in a pot, six different buttons or coloured counters.

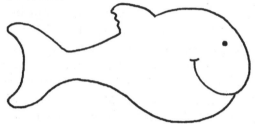

Preparation

Mount the photocopiable sheet (preferably enlarged) on to card and cover with plastic film (optional). Cut out the fish from the coloured paper using a simple template (see diagram).

What to do

Give each child a button or counter and let them choose or throw the dice to decide who should go first (the highest number goes first). When it is their turn, each child puts their counter on **start** which shows them to take two fish straight away. They then throw the dice from the pot and move their counter as many squares as the number on the dice. If they land on a square with fish they pick up that number of fish. If they land on a square with a creature who eats fish they give one fish back. How many fish do they have each when they reach the **end**?

Discussion

A fish is an animal that cannot breathe out of water. It doesn't breathe through a nose like we do, but through gills which are little covered openings on either side of its head. The fish takes a great big gulp of water and uses the oxygen (gas) in the water to breathe. It pushes the water back out through its gills. Why does a goldfish keep opening its mouth as it swims around? A fish uses its fins to swim and to keep it the right way up. It can sense along its side when it is going to bump into rocks and other fish. Fish eat smaller fish, insects and water-plants for food. If the water where they live is too hot or too cold it makes them slow or sickly. What would make the water too hot or cold? [The sun or freezing conditions.]

Follow-up activities

✧ Make a fish puppet by drawing round your hand on to card. Cut out the hand shape (an adult may need to do this). Draw a mouth and eye, and colour the finger 'fins'. Tape a lolly stick on to the back. (See illustration below.)

✧ Add some 'hand' fish to 'The Deep Blue Sea' display on page 60.

✧ Move around like fish with popping eyes, waggling 'fins' and opening and closing mouths. What happens at feeding time?

✧ Read the poem 'Who Lives in the Sea?' page 68 and sing 'What's that Bobbing in the Sea' page 86.

✧ How many different types of fish can you name?

SNAPPING JAWS

Objective

English – To play a guessing game based on animals which live in water.

Group size

The whole group.

What you need

Pictures or photos of the following animals: a crocodile, a hippopotamus, a seal, a turtle.

Discussion

Many animals have their homes in water and only come out for food or to have their babies. A crocodile has eyes and nostrils on the roof of its head so that it can hide under water but still see above it and breathe. It uses its tail to swim and its legs for moving on land. They can be very long (six metres). Why does it have very sharp teeth? (To eat people!) A hippopotamus looks like a wrinkly barrel with short legs and big clumsy feet. It loves to laze and swim in the water all day, and can even walk along the bottom of a lake. Why does the mother carry her baby on her back? (Because it can't swim.) A seal can not move easily on land but it is a wonderful swimmer with its powerful flippers. It can go to sleep under the water for about 10 minutes before it has to come up for air. Seal babies are called pups and are white when they are born. What noise do seals make? (Oink oink.) Why does a turtle have a shell and webbed feet?

(To protect it and to help it swim.) It has a sharp horny beak instead of teeth and some like being buried in shallow mud. Baby turtles hatch out of eggs which have been laid in holes on the beach.

What to do

After the discussion show the children the animal pictures one at a time and ask them what they can remember from their discussion about the animals. Shuffle the pictures, choose one and don't let them see which it is. Ask them to guess which animal is on your picture from the clues you are going to give them. Proceed to give one clue at a time until the children have guessed the right animal. Now it is the winner's turn to choose an animal and to give the clues to the others. Repeat the game with all the animals and perhaps guess some other animals which live in water.

Follow-up activities

✧ Draw a make-up animal together. Someone draw a body, someone else some legs/ flippers, a head and so on. Give the animal a name such as 'turtledile' or 'hipposeal'.

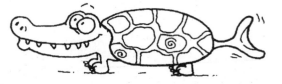

✧ Sing the 'Hippopotamus song' from *Apusskidu* (A&C Black).
✧ Perform the action poem 'Water' on page 67.
✧ Move around like one of the water animals. Can anyone guess which one you are?

WATER THE CRESS

Objective

Science – To investigate whether seeds can grow without water.

Group size

Six children.

What you need

Six thick paper towels, a jug of water, a packet of cress seeds, three dishes (or polystyrene food trays), newspaper, a kitchen tray, three marking labels and a pencil.

What to do

Ask three children each to fold two paper towels together in half and half again, then place them into the three dishes. Pour some water into two of the dishes, pour off the excess and keep the two towels damp until seeds have sprouted.

Tip a few of the cress seeds into the palms of the other three children's hands and show them how to lift some seeds out of their palm to place them on top of the towels in the dishes – including the dry one. Label each dish appropriately – 'wet' or 'dry'. Place the dishes on the tray, cover them all with newspaper, and leave them in an airy place. Look at the seeds after 24 hours to see if anything has happened. Once the sprouted seeds are 2.5cm long (four days) remove the newspaper. Ensure that one dish of growing cress is kept thoroughly moist at all times. Let the other 'wet' one dry out and notice what happens to the cress that was growing in it.

Discussion

What happened to the seeds after 24 hours and over the next few days? Why didn't the seeds on the dry cloth start to sprout? All living things need water to begin to grow. What happened to the seeds which started to grow but were not watered? If a living thing has its water supply cut off it will wilt and die. Point out to the children that they have a responsibility to water seeds which they have sown. Similarly if they keep pets they need to make sure that the pets always have water available to drink.

Follow-up activities

✧ Write the first letter of your name on to a folded paper towel. Wet it and sow seeds on to the outline of the letter. See your initial growing on the paper.
✧ Grow wild bird seeds on some different absorbent surfaces such as, cardboard, orange peel, a (clean!) nappy, some sand.
✧ Slice the top off a carrot and a parsnip and place them face down in a saucer of water to start them growing again.
✧ Sing 'A Man with a Watering Can' on page 84.
✧ Read the story 'Ellie's Magic Roof Garden' on page 79.

LIKE MARBLES

Objective

Art – To find out that some things will not mix with water and to produce a marble effect picture.

Group size

Four children.

What you need

Some vegetable cooking oil, a large glass bowl half filled with water, two kitchen forks, coloured waterproof inks (special marbling ink is available from educational suppliers and art shops), a baking tray half filled with water (or polystyrene food tray), a piece of paper for each child, damp cloth for spills, a few marbles.

What to do

Pour some cooking oil into the bowl of water and let the children take it in turns to try and mix the oil and water with a fork. For the picture, drip some drops of different coloured inks on to the water in the tray. Let each child gently stir the ink with the fork and watch the colours blend, swirl, ooze and dot until a pleasing pattern has been made. To capture this pattern, lay a piece of paper on top of the floating inks for half a minute then peel it off quickly. Dry it flat so that the colours don't run. If thin absorbent paper has been used, the patterns will look lovely if fixed to a window pane. You may need to add more ink as other children do the activity. Compare the swirling pictures to the marbles.

Discussion

What happened when the oil and water were stirred in the bowl ? How can you tell which is heavier, oil or water? (Oil is lighter and floats.) Sometimes ships at sea spill their oil which won't mix with the water. The oil floats to the beach and leaves thick tarry blobs on the sand. What happens to the sea birds in an oily sea? (The oil sticks to their wings and prevents them flying.) Also, fish fins get stuck. What other things don't mix with sea water? Discuss the litter which people leave behind them (drink cans, picnic remains). Talk about some remarkable things that get washed up from the sea, like old boots and bedsteads!

Follow-up activities

✧ Find out if these will mix with water – syrup, vinegar, ice-cream, flour, brown sugar, rice, shampoo, sawdust, newspaper.

✧ Play a game of marbles: roll your marbles to hit another one. (Marbles can be dangerous if left on the floor.)

✧ Make a 'litter-can man'. Pleat a piece of paper and cut it into four strips for his arms and legs. Stick them on to an empty drink can and give him a face.

✧ Show how litter spoils the beach on the seaside display in chapter 7 (see page 61).

✧ Move like a sea-bird covered in oil.

✧ Sing 'The Wombling Song' in *Apusskidu* (A&C Black).

CHAPTER 6
WORKING WITH WATER

Some people's jobs involve working with water. Firemen use it to control fires, lifeboat workers use it to reach people in trouble at sea, fish catchers provide us with fish to eat, and water workers re-cycle our water and keep it clean. In the past, pirates and train drivers also used to work with water.

FULL STEAM AHEAD

Objective

History – To gain an understanding of how trains in the past used steam power, and to play a game of trains.

Group size

The whole group.

What you need

A whistle, access to and use of a boiling ring either gas or electricity, whistling or metal lidded kettle (an electric kettle will not do), a jug of cold water.

What to do

Ask the children to blow on their hands then show them how you can blow through the kettle's whistle or the holes in the kettle lid. Three-quarters fill the kettle with water and put it on the heat (supervise at all times). When it has been boiling long enough for the steam to build up inside it will either whistle or the lid will rattle.

Having explained to the children how trains used to be powered (see 'Discussion' below) let them have a chance of 'letting off steam' themselves! Choose one child to be the engine and some others can be the carriages. They can run round holding on to each other's waists. Don't forget they will need signals, a station guard and a tunnel (of other children's arms).

Discussion

First make sure the children realise the kettle will be very hot, unlike a plastic kettle, and they should not touch.

What did it feel like when the children blew on their hands? Boiling water gives off steam (tiny little droplets of water) which can be seen as it rushes to get out anywhere it can. Steam will push hard against anything that is in its way. It pushes through the whistle and makes it blow or it steams through the holes in the kettle's lid and tries to push it off. A long time ago trains carried coal to heat water and make steam. The train driver used this steam to make the wheels of his train move round. What makes passenger trains move nowadays? (Electricity.)

Follow-up activities

✧ Add some sound effects to your train movement: brush a fully opened newspaper to make the sound of hissing steam; give the guard a whistle; drum two empty tins with teaspoons to make the rhythmical sound of wheels on rails; say 'chug chug chugga chug'.
✧ Make a train picture using some gummed sticky shapes (see diagram above).
✧ Say the rhyme 'I'm a little teapot' in *Round and Round the Garden* by Sarah Williams (OUP).
✧ Sing 'The Runaway Train' from *Ta-ra-ra boom-de-ay* (A & C Black).

HOSE AND LADDERS

Objective

Physical Education – To look at jets of water and for the children to move their bodies in curves like those jets.

Group size

The whole group.

What you need

A kitchen colander, a large empty plastic drink bottle, an ear dropper, an oral medicine syringe (the last two can be obtained from a chemist), a washing-up liquid bottle, skewer or metal knitting needle, large jug.

Preparation

An adult can use the skewer to pierce holes in a diagonal line along the length of the large bottle (see diagram).

What to do

This activity will be much more successful if done outside, but is possible to do over a sink or the water tray. Pour water through the colander and watch the shape it makes as it comes out of the holes. Pour water very quickly into the bottle to fill it before it empties! Notice what happens to the water as it gradually stops coming out of each hole.

Fill the dropper and the syringe with water and then force the water out. Finally, fill the squeezy bottle with water, replace the cap and squeeze the bottle to form a jet. Watch the shape the jet makes. Ask the children to find ways to make curved shapes with their bodies, like the curves they have seen made by the water.

Discussion

Did the children notice that the water came out of all the containers in curves? Which containers made the smallest and which the largest curves? When the water spurted out of the bottle with holes were the curves all the same? When the squeezy bottle was pressed it forced water out fast and strong and made the biggest jet. Fire fighters use pumps which force water out of their hoses very strongly and quickly. These powerful water jets can reach up to a great height when tall buildings catch on fire.

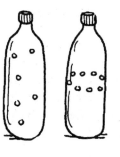

Follow-up activities

◇ Pour water into bottles with a single hole, a circle of holes or random holes. Tilt the bottles to switch the holes 'on' and 'off'.

◇ Squirt water from squeezy bottles aiming at an upturned bucket. Keep moving back to see if your jet can still 'touch' the bucket.

◇ Sew curves by joining points (equally spaced and numbered) along two lines which meet at an angle (see illustration above).

◇ Find a fire hydrant in the street (H on a yellow metal wall-plate) and make a paper rubbing using the side of a thick wax crayon.

◇ Say the poem 'Water's For...' on page 71.

◇ Sing the song 'The Fireman' from *Apusskidu* (A&C Black).

DRIP, DRIP, DRIP

Objective

English – To play with pieces of pipe and practise using the opposites of words.

Group size

Eight children.

What you need

A large bucket, an assortment of pieces of piping of different lengths, diameters and materials – copper and plastic. Several off-cuts of plastic drain pipes of different widths and lengths – from a friendly plumber or DIY enthusiast! If you are unable to get real piping, make do with cardboard tubes, pieces of hose, rubber and plastic tubing, straws, plastic drink bottles with their tops and bottoms removed.

What to do

Let the children handle the pieces of piping – fitting them into each other or standing them on end. Select two pieces of pipe and describe them – for example 'wide' and 'narrow'. Describe other pieces of pipe arranging them in pairs as follows:
✧ long and short
✧ many and few
✧ rough and smooth
✧ straight and curved
✧ hard and soft
✧ big and little
✧ thick and thin
✧ old and new

Use other pipes in pairs with the empty bucket to position them:
✧ right and left
✧ on top and underneath
✧ above and below
✧ inside and outside
✧ near and far
✧ back and front
✧ in front and behind
  When the children are familiar with the opposites, play a game of 'who can be the first to bring me' – a long and a short piece, a straight and a curved piece and so on.

Discussion

Drainpipes are used to channel rain down from our roofs. Other pipes are used to move water in and out of our houses. What kind of water comes into the house (clean), what kind goes out (dirty / used) and what kind goes round and round (central heating)? Plumbers lay the pipes in position and connect them all together. If pipes aren't joined properly dirt can get in or water can leak out. What do we do when we want a drink of water? Turning on the tap is like taking the top off a bottle – the water is already waiting in the pipe. If you don't turn the tap off properly it drips.

Follow-up activities

✧ What water noises do you hear in your house?
✧ Arrange the pipes in length order, or order of diameter size.
✧ Find pipes inside the house and see what they are connected to (heating, sinks).
✧ Make pipe prints on paper by pressing the ends on to a sponge soaked in paint.
✧ Say the poem 'The Central heating' on page 70.
✧ Read the story *Mrs Plug the Plumber* by Janet and Allan Ahlberg (Puffin).
✧ Make a 'House Pipes' display (see page 59).
✧ Sing 'Johnny lost his marble' from *The Funny Family* (Ward Lock).

CAUGHT IN A NET

Objective

Design and Technology – To design and select the appropriate materials to make a fish card.

Group size

Six children.

What you need

Fruit nets from supermarkets, or larger net sacks from a greengrocer. For each child – scissors, adhesive and scrapers, paper, pencils, a piece of A4 size card, crayons and felt-tipped pens. A collection of decorating material such as seeds (especially honesty seeds), eggshell (baked), pasta, foil, sequin strip, buttons, glitter, coloured Cellophane paper, tissue paper circles, coloured gummed paper.

Preparation

Cut the cards to 15cm wide (still A4 long) and then fold them in half lengthways.

What to do

Ask the children to practise drawing fish and then choose, cut (if necessary) and arrange what they want to use for the fish scales. When they are pleased with their plan they can draw their chosen fish outline on to the card and stick down overlapping scales, starting from the head. Remember to give the fish an eye and mouth. Cut out a piece of netting which is bigger than the fish

and stick it over the fish on the card. The children can write 'from ... (name)' inside the card and give it to their friend or family.

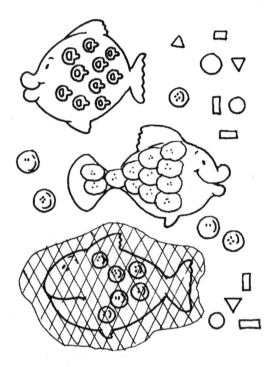

Discussion

People catch fish with a fishing rod and line or by using nets. A special ship called a trawler drags fishing nets through the sea. The fish get caught but the water is able to get through the holes in the net. If only big fish are wanted, the net has big enough holes to let the little fish escape. To catch fish with a rod and line you need to sit very still at the water's edge. Why do people who fish have to be very patient? Sometimes people throw a line out from a boat floating in deep water. How can you tell when you have caught a fish? (You can feel it tugging on the end of the line.)

Follow-up activities

✧ Play a game of magnetic fish. Cut out fish shapes, put a paper-clip on the end of each and catch them using a magnet on a string.
✧ Cut out some decorated fish, string them up and make a mobile.
✧ Sing 'Michael Row the Boat Ashore' from *Ta-ra-ra boom-de-ay* (A&C Black).
✧ Say the nursery rhyme '1,2,3,4,5, Once I caught a fish alive'.
✧ Add some fish to 'The Deep Blue Sea' display (see page 60).

JOLLY ROGER

Objective

History – To discover that in the past pirates robbed ships at sea and to make a pirate's flag.

Group size

Six children.

What you need

A piece of thick card 18cm x 12cm, a craft knife, black paper (see 'Preparation'), six pieces of white chalk, a two-hole punch, paper-clips, six thin sticks 30cm long (from garden centres), sticky tape.

Preparation

Draw the outline of a skull and crossbones on the card and cut out the shaded shapes (see diagram) to make a stencil. Cut the black paper into six pieces size 18cm × 12cm.

What to do

Let the children use the hole punch, lining up one long side of their piece of black paper. Fix this black paper underneath the stencil with four paper-clips. One child can draw round the stencil outline with the chalk. They then pass the stencil to the next child. The children should chalk in the outlines of the skull and crossbones being careful not to smudge. For the eyes they will need to lick their finger and make two dabs in the right place (the chalk will come off). To complete the flag push the stick in at one hole and out at the other, lining it up with the top of the flag. Tape the stick at the back to stop it slipping.

Discussion

A long time ago pirates would jump from their own ships on to smaller ships and rob them. What sort of things would they take (gold, silver, guns)? Sometimes the pirates would capture the whole ship for themselves and would get rid of the ships'

sailors by making them walk off the end of a plank to drown in the sea. Why did the pirates have a picture of a skull and crossbones on their flag? (To frighten other sailors.) Their flag was called the 'Jolly Roger'. Women who wanted to be pirates dressed up to look like men pirates.

Follow-up activities

✧ Walk along a piece of board to play at 'walking the plank'.
✧ Read the story of *Peter Pan* Ladybird Disney and find out how Captain Hook lost his arm.
✧ Dress up as pirates using a spotted headscarf, a black eye-patch and some curtain-ring earrings.
✧ Sing the song 'Terrors of the Sea' on page 86.

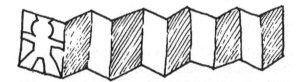

✧ Make a line of dancing sailors. Fold some paper into a concertina. Draw a sailor on the top fold with arms and legs outstretched to each edge of the paper. Cut out the sailor (not the end of his arms) holding all the folds of paper together – open them out and see all the sailors dancing.

HIGH LIGHTS

Objective

Religious Education — To be aware that some people are brave enough to risk their lives for others; and to make a lighthouse.

Group size

Six children.

What you need

A long cardboard tube (from foil) and ping-pong ball for each child, a variety of thick felt-tipped pens, Plasticine or Blu-Tack.

What to do

Tell the children the story of Grace Darling who lived with her family in a lighthouse (*Children's Encyclopaedia Britannica*).

One night there was a terrible storm and a steamship smashed into some rocks and was wrecked. The sea was too rough for the lifeboats to come out from the shore, so Grace helped her father to row their small boat to the shipwrecked sailors. It was a terrible struggle to row the boat against the strong waves and not to hit the rocks in the water. Even though Grace was not very strong she managed to look after the boat while her father helped the injured men to get into it. She and her father were given gold medals for being so brave and caring.

To make a lighthouse show the children where to draw windows and a door, starting about one third up on their cardboard tube. Draw some steps from the bottom of the tube up to the door. Rest the ping-pong ball in the top of the tube as the search light. Wedge it in place with Plasticine.

Discussion

A lighthouse is built on the coastline or on rocks out at sea. At night it flashes its light every half minute to warn passing ships that they are near to a rocky area. Why would it be dangerous for the ships to come too close? Why isn't the door to some lighthouses built at the bottom of the tower? The lower part of the lighthouse is often built in the sea so that small boats can bring things to the people who live in the lighthouse. What kind of things would they need? (Food, water, letters, newspapers, medicines, clothes, toys.)

Follow-up activities

✧ Use Plasticine to stand your lighthouse in a foil tray. Heap large pebbles round it at the bottom and fill the tray with water — a lighthouse at sea.
✧ Flash a torch every half minute like a lighthouse does. You will need a watch with a second hand.
✧ Join the 'Storm Force' club to help save people's lives. It is the young peoples' part of the Royal National Lifeboat Institution (address on page 96).
✧ Say the poem 'The Lighthouse' from *The Book of a Thousand Poems* (Collins).
✧ Sing 'A sailor went to sea' from *The Funny Family* (A&C Black).

MUDDY MIXTURE

Objective

Science – To experiment and find out how dirty water can be cleaned.

Group size

Six children.

What you need

A bucket and trowel, garden soil, fallen leaves and twigs, gravel and garden stones, water, three drinking glasses, a sieve, a tablespoon, litre size glass jug, two one litre size clear plastic drink bottles (for example, from soda water), strong scissors, one coffee filter cone (or clean paper nappy liner), the foot cut off some tights.

Preparation

Cut right through the plastic bottles about one third down from the top. Invert the neck pieces inside the base pieces to form two funnels. Line one funnel with the nylon 'foot' and the other with the filter cone.

What to do

If possible let the children collect the 'ingredients' for the muddy mixture from outside (soil, twigs, pine needles and so on) and put them into the bucket. Add enough water to stir it into a really messy sludge!

Spoon some sludge into a glass for comparison later. Rest the sieve in the glass jug and pour enough mixture through it to nearly fill the jug.

You may need to use a glass to do this rather than pour from the bucket which may be too heavy. Make sure you include some sludge from the bottom of the bucket.

When the sieve has finished dripping, rest it on the bucket and slowly pour some mixture from the jug into both the lined funnels. Ensure that the mixture only goes through the nylon and the paper cone, and not down the sides. Compare all the stages of filtering with a glass of clean tap water.

Muddy mix   using a sieve

using nylon tights   using a filter cone   clear tap water

Discussion

Did the sieve clean the water? What was left in the sieve? Why was the water from the paper filter cleaner than from the nylon filter? The filters with the smallest holes trap the most dirt. Even the cleanest filtered water is far too dirty to be safe to drink. Whenever we use water we dirty it and this dirty water leaves our houses through pipes. It travels through big underground pipes called sewers to the sewage works. The water is cleaned before it goes back into the rivers and sea. Water that is stored in reservoirs needs more cleaning at the waterworks before we can use it.

Follow-up activities

✧ Examine the filter paper and nylon foot when they are dry.
✧ Leave a glass of muddy water to settle having stirred it. What happens?
✧ Water is precious – how many ways can you think of saving it? (Rain barrels, not leaving taps running and turning them off properly.)
✧ Make a display of House Pipes (see page 59).
✧ Say the poem 'Voices of Water' on page 74.
✧ Flush a lavatory and ask the children to describe what happens to the water – it twists and swirls.

SUNKEN TREASURE

Objective

Physical Education — To move around obstacles like divers who are looking for sunken treasure.

Group size

The whole group.

What you need

Three very large deep cardboard boxes, three or four cushions, five or six carpet tiles, a car tyre, hoop, chairs, table and dust-sheet, one stout bamboo cane or long handled brush, small decorative box containing some plastic jewellery.

Preparation

Hide the box of 'treasure' but not too obviously!

What to do

Let the children help to arrange the obstacles on the floor — include any climbing equipment you have. Open up both ends of the boxes and lay them end to end to form a tunnel. Cover the table with the sheet leaving an opening — to be like a cave. Wedge the hoop between some chairs so that the children can scramble through it. Spread carpet tiles for stepping stones. Lay the tyre flat so the children can walk round the rim as if balancing on rocks. Rest the cane across two chairs for the children to squeeze under. Arrange groups of chairs to be climbed on, under and through. Scatter the cushions like jellyfish and octopuses. Ask the children to 'swim' around this underwater scene searching for the box of hidden treasure. Remind them that it's dark under water so they must be careful not to get stuck in a cave, grabbed by an octopus or stung by a jellyfish!

Discussion

Some deep sea divers search for treasure from wrecked ships. Sometimes they repair the underneath of floating ships. Some divers are part of the police force and dive to rescue people or cars which are stuck under water. Deep sea divers wear special clothes — rubber suits and helmets attached to breathing equipment. Why do they wear weighted boots? (To keep upright.) Skin divers do not go down very deep and therefore only need to wear flippers and mask. Some divers gather natural sponges (which are living sea animals) and others collect oysters from the sea bed. Oysters are shellfish which spin beautiful pearls inside their shells.

Follow-up activities

◇ Give a copy of photocopiable page 95 and some coloured counters to each child. Ask them to place a counter in the position you describe, for example 'place a blue counter above the diver'. Use other positions such as on, in, below, next to, at the side of. Vary the activity by actually drawing counters in the positions.

◇ Make 'The Deep Blue Sea' display on page 60.

◇ Arrange a simple treasure hunt using pictures and arrows for clues.

◇ Sing the song 'Yellow Submarine' from *Apusskidu* (A&C Black).

◇ Make a 'feely' bag with things from the interest table. Take turns to guess what you are touching in the bag.

CHAPTER 7
DISPLAYS

Displays are your shop window telling visitors what you are doing in your group. Ensure that they are clearly titled and labelled, and talk about them with the children. Plan the displays carefully, arranging them with drawing pins before the final stapling.

HOUSE PIPES

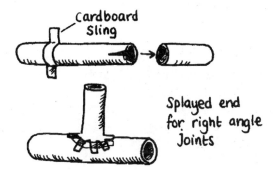

What you need

Pale coloured backing paper to fit display area, four white sheets of A4 card, thick marker pens, felt-tipped pens, pencils, corrugated cardboard, scissors, an assortment of long cardboard tubes, sticky tape, card for 'slings', drawing pins, staple gun, adhesive, thin brown cardboard sheets to roll into large tubes, a very small piece of polystyrene.

What to do

Ask four children to draw one room each on the white cards, for example a bedroom with a wash-hand basin; a bathroom with a lavatory, wash-hand basin, bath and/or shower; a kitchen with a sink; a garage with a washing machine. Staple these four rooms on to the lined display area, leaving enough room between the floors to 'lay' some pipes. Cut a roof shape from the corrugated card and staple it so that it is three dimensional (polystyrene behind) and overhangs the house. Connect the cardboard tubes by making an indented 'V' shaped channel at one end of the tubes and pushing them into one another. Staple the tubes (or use cardboard slings) to lead away from the household waste outlets (draw these). Make a large sewer pipe out of the cardboard sheets and run it under the house. Join the down spouts at right angles to the sewer by fringing and splaying the ends of the tubes. Tape the fringes in place.

Discussion

The discussions in activities 'Drip, drip, drip' on page 53 and 'Muddy Mixture' on page 57, are relevant to this display.

Follow-up work

✧ Remove a section of the display roof and add a cardboard box for a cold water storage tank.
✧ Split some cardboard tubes lengthways and staple them under the roof as guttering.
✧ Examine a disconnected tap to see how it works.
✧ Remove the lid off a toilet cistern, flush it and watch how the ball-cock moves.

THE DEEP BLUE SEA

What you need

A strip of pale blue backing paper for the top third of the display area and dark blue backing paper for the lower two thirds, black and white paper for drawings, black marker pen, pencils, scissors, felt-tipped pens, adhesive and scrapers, craft knife, two empty black camera film canisters, cord or plastic tubing, empty fluted plastic dessert moulds, an egg carton, thick wool or string, dark tissue paper, bubble wrap, green paint and brush, ice-lolly sticks and bits of balsa wood, stapler and drawing pins.

What to do

Ask some children to draw wavy lines with the black marker pen across the light blue paper to look like waves. Staple this and the other background paper to the display area. Draw and cut out the divers and staple them to the dark blue paper. Use a blue paper 'sling' to fix the film canisters to the divers' backs to look like cylinders of air. Connect these to their mouths with the pieces of cord or plastic tubing. Cut out single egg cartons and glue eight strands of thick wool inside each to hang down like the tentacles of octopuses. Draw their eyes and fix them to the display. Add fluted moulds to look like jellyfish. Screw up some tissue

paper rocks and staple them on the sea bottom. Cut irregular sized pieces of bubble-wrap, paint them green and fix them to look like floating seaweed. Draw and cut out a treasure chest to fix to the bottom of the display. Fix ice-lolly sticks and bits of balsa wood near to the treasure chest to look like a wrecked ship.

Discussion

This display links with the activities in 'Bobbing up and down' (page 23), 'Catch a fish alive' (page 47) and 'Sunken treasure' (page 58).

Follow-up work

✧ Decorate some fish (see page 54) and add them to the display. Some fish can't be seen in the water because they are camouflaged, others all move together in a shoal.
✧ Make a necklace from cut coloured straws or pieces of macaroni threaded on to a shoelace. Cover some copper money with gold and silver paper to look like valuable coins in the wreck. Add the jewellery and coins to the display, to spill out of the treasure chest.
✧ Draw a submarine for the display. Submarines can see what's going on above the water by using a periscope (a system of mirrors and prisms which reflect light).

BESIDE THE SEASIDE

What you need

Three coloured strips of frieze paper to fit the display area, light blue, dark blue and buff, paint for finger painting waves (see page 20), a packet of sand paper (from pet shops for lining budgie cages), black marker pen, blue ribbon (florist's type), grey sugar paper, silver foil, scissors, a few real shells, Plasticine, thin paper, wax crayons, staples, drawing pins, paper, pencils and felt-tipped pens, adhesive.

What to do

Cut the bottom edge of the dark blue frieze paper unevenly to look like the water's edge and finger paint waves right across the paper. Staple this and the other background paper on to the display area – light blue for the sky, dark blue for the sea and buff for the beach. Cut and arrange the sand paper pieces to look like a sand-castle with turrets. Add extra sand pies at the side. Stick the blue ribbon round the castle base to look like water coming from the sea and filling a moat. Cut out some foil starfish. Make some shell rubbings. Secure the shell firmly on a blob of Plasticine, hold paper over it and rub with the side of a wax crayon until the shell pattern appears. Cut these patterns out (in the shape of the shell) and use them and the starfish to decorate on and around the sand-castle. Cut rock outlines out of the grey paper and stick on strips of foil to look like rock pools glinting in the sun. Fix them to the display. Add drawings of children playing with buckets and spades.

Discussion

See the activities 'Dipping dips' (page 20), 'Beach pebbles' (page 21) and 'Like marbles' (page 50) which all link with this display.

Follow-up work

✧ Discuss the purpose of moats and drawbridges on real castles.
✧ Make cocktail stick flags to represent the nationalities of the children in your group. Push the flags into the top of the sand-castle.
✧ Make some boat silhouettes with black paper and stick them far out at sea.
✧ Read the poems 'Days by the Sea' on page 67 and 'Ice lollies' on page 74.

IT'S SOAKING

What you need

A gauze bandage, a roll of toilet tissue and kitchen towel (near to the end), a roll of cotton wool, thick natural (not nylon) string, a piece of clean towelling nappy, a piece of pure cotton fabric, newspaper, washing-up cloth, large pot of a brightly coloured 'runny' paint and a thick paint brush, large flat baking tray (or polystyrene food tray), two black bin bags, scissors, drawing pins, stapler, sticky tape, rubber bands, a broad marker pen, card, pale blue background paper.

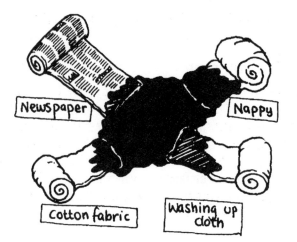

What to do

Make the nappy, newspaper, washing-up cloth and cotton fabric into narrow rolls by cutting and sticking. Cover a large table with the bin bags and place the baking tray in the middle. Pour plenty of paint into the baking tray and arrange all the different rolls around the edge of the table. Unwind them until one end reaches into the paint tray in the middle. When they have finished absorbing paint (each will have a different rate) lift the soaking ends out of the tray and leave them on the bin bag to dry. Paint a generous 'puddle' of the same paint on to card. Cut round it and staple this 'puddle' to the middle of the background paper in the display area. When all the rolls are dry, carefully lift them up, pin them in a circular arrangement (as on the table) on to the wall letting the paint end reach the 'puddle'. Label all the different materials.

Discussion

Which materials absorbed the most paint from the puddle? (Cotton materials suck up the most water.) If you put grease (Vaseline) on the materials will they still absorb the paint puddle?

Follow-up work

✧ When is it important to use materials which soak up lots of liquid? (For drying, babies' nappies, and 'accidents'!)

✧ Test other things for absorption — polythene bags (closely supervised), wellingtons, leather, wool, carpet, wood, coins.

✧ Fold a paper towel into four and into four again. Dip each folded corner quickly into four different saucers of coloured water (use food colouring). When the towel is dry open it up and see the symmetrical patterns.

✧ Scribble yellow wax crayon over a piece of paper and then paint the paper — what happens?

RAIN RAIN GO AWAY!

What you need

Blue background paper, black and dark blue paper, orange card and orange tones of paper and fabric, scissors, adhesive, pencils, net curtain wire and hooks, clothes pegs, a pair of child's wellington boots, child's raincoat and hat, a child's umbrella, rain-hood, black marker pens, colourful wallpaper or gift wrapping paper, pipe cleaners or bendy straws, stapler.

What to do

Cut the orange card into a circle for the sun and ask the children to cut and stick pieces of orange paper and fabric in collage-style on the circle. Staple the sun on to the blue paper display area. Cut two stout posts from black paper and staple them to either side of the display. Screw in the hooks for the curtain line at the top of each post and fix the line securely across. Peg up all the rain wear and hook the umbrella on the line. Cut some puddles out of the dark blue paper and position them under each article which is hanging on the line. Ask the children to draw raindrops dripping from the clothes to the puddles. Make an umbrella and wellington boot template and show them how to draw and cut round it on the fancy wallpaper. Staple a pipe cleaner to each umbrella to make a handle. Staple these wellies and umbrellas as a border round the display. Label everything clearly.

Discussion

See the 'Raindrops' activity on page 13 which links with this display.

Follow-up work

✧ On a rainy day check that all the children's wellingtons are named. Throw them into the middle of the room. When you say 'go' the children have to find and pair their own wellingtons. Point out that each child has two wellies but only one pair.

✧ Think of all the sounds that are made with water and write each one on a 'puddle' – roar (waves), gush, drip, trickle, bubble, clink (ice), crunch (on snow), gulp (drinking), suck, lap (dog), splash, gurgle, hiss (steam).

✧ Read the poem 'Blue Wellies Yellow Wellies' on page 73.

CHAPTER 8
ASSEMBLIES

This chapter gives ideas for assemblies or group sharing times based on the theme of Water. Children can be given opportunities to consider the importance of water in our everyday lives and its role in many different religions.

WATER FOR LIFE

The focus for this approach is on water as an essential part of life.

It involves the children in drawing on experiences they may have already had during other activities, particularly in science, where there are opportunities to discover what happens to plants which are deprived of water. These should have alerted them to the role water has in sustaining and maintaining a variety of life forms, including themselves!

The assembly will begin to lay the foundations for a future understanding of how water is used as a symbol of life and new growth in a variety of religious traditions, especially Christianity.

Introduction

Play some appropriate music as the children enter the assembly area; Handel's *Water Music* is an obvious choice! Begin by asking them to recall as many different ways in which water is essential to life; list these on a flip chart. Give the children a visual reference by contrasting a picture of a desert landscape with a leafy, woodland scene.

Encourage the children to present their own art work, perhaps depicting themselves enjoying a long glass of cold squash on a hot and sunny day.

Ensure that the children have understood that water is necessary for life, and explain that this is why Christian people use it as a sign of life in some of their most important ceremonies.

Activity

Display some pictures/artefacts relating to Christian baptism. Include contribution from the children. They can be used to initiate a discussion on christening. Give them opportunities to share relevant experiences they have had (for example, a baby sister's or brother's christening). A group of children could present a pre-planned drama or role-play in which they depict what happens at an infant christening; different children take different roles, including parents, godparents, family, friends and even the priest or minister! Particular emphasis should be given to the moment when water is poured over the baby's head as a sign of new life.

If a drama or role-play cannot be prepared, some children may have video footage of their own baptisms which can be shown instead.

Reflection

Encourage the children to think carefully about the importance of water in their own lives and in the world around them. It should be remembered that other Christian denominations may have different practices or beliefs about baptism.

> ### Prayer
>
> Some children may wish to thank God for the water which is essential in their lives and pray for those who are deprived of it, such as children in some parts of Africa.

WATER FOR CLEANSING

The focus for this approach is on the cleansing qualities of water.

They will be drawing on experiences they may have had during other activities, particularly in science, design and technology, language work and in the context of personal and social development.

These activities should have contributed to their understanding of the many different ways in which water is used to clean both themselves and the things around them.

The assembly will lay the foundation for a later understanding of the way in which water is used as a symbol of spiritual cleansing in a variety of faith traditions, particularly Islam.

Introduction

Begin by inviting the children to identify the many occasions when water is used for cleansing – these should include bath time, laundering clothes, mopping the kitchen floor, preparing to eat a meal, a visit to the car wash or a trip to the hairdressers.

Ask the children to illustrate their examples by doing paintings, drawings, collages or models, or by performing simple mimes, dramas or role-plays.

Discuss with the children why it is important to be clean and ask them to identify occasions when it is particularly appropriate to look as neat and clean as possible, such as a birthday party or a visit

to granny and grandad. In a small group, it may be possible to encourage spontaneous responses from individual children, but in a larger gathering some preparation may be necessary.

Activity

Emphasise that people use water to make themselves clean before doing something important – for some people, saying their prayers is very important, so they take great care to wash themselves properly first. This is particularly true for Muslim people.

If there is a Muslim in the group – perhaps a child, a parent, or a member of staff – he or she may be willing to demonstrate to the others the way in which a devout Muslim performs *wudu* (ritual washing) before prayer. It may be possible to contact a local Muslim representative to do this, but make sure that the visitor is able to speak to the children in an appropriate way.

Alternatively, you could inform the children about what happens by making use of pictures, posters, video material and other resources (see recommended materials on page 96).

Reflection

Ask the children to think about the many different ways in which water features in their lives each day and encourage them to consider how it can be used sparingly and sensibly.

You could accompany the reflection with a recording made by you of running water playing quietly in the background.

Prayer

Either include a Muslim prayer at this point or invite those who wish to do so to thank God for the gift of water and the many different ways in which it can be used to make the world a better place.

Rhymes and Songs

If you wish to continue the Muslim theme, read nursery rhymes which cover Muslim beliefs in a simple way (see recommended materials on page 96). Alternatively, you could sing the Christian song 'Water of Life' from the BBC publication *Come and Praise* or select a song from the collection featured within this book.

WATER IN THE NATURAL WORLD

The focus for this approach is on water in the natural world.

Before this assembly takes place, give the children opportunities to develop their awareness of the presence of water in their immediate environment and beyond. These could include the monitoring of rainfall; an exploration of pond life; stories, rhymes and poems about the seaside; the making of toy boats to sail (supervised) on a stream.

The assembly will help children to appreciate the variety of forms which water takes in the natural world and lay the foundations for an awareness of relevant environmental issues.

Include some simple safety instructions (such as never going into water unless an adult is there; always wearing wellington boots when playing in water) and emphasise that, although water activities are great fun, they can also be very dangerous.

Introduction

Begin by asking the children to share their classroom-based work experiences of water with one another – songs can be sung, poems and rhymes can be recited and pictures, posters, models, charts and graphs can be displayed.

Encourage the children to list as many different examples as possible of water in the natural world; their responses could be recorded on a flip chart or presented in pictorial form and might include lakes, streams, ponds and rain water, as well as the sea.

Activity

Arrange the gathering area with a large, open space in the centre – this should feature representations of the sea, a river and a pond.

Swish blue and green fabrics across the floor to represent the sea, and let the children play percussion instruments to create the sound of waves; fasten together silver paper collages to suggest the shiny surface of a pond; let children wearing streamers made of ribbons or crêpe paper wave them to show the movements of a river.

Ask two children to demonstrate the do's and don'ts' of playing near and in water, perhaps through short role-plays they have devised themselves in previous sessions. Invite the audience to identify the actions which are appropriate and those which are inappropriate in and around water.

Reflection

Encourage all the children to think about the importance of taking care of water in the environment. Show them some colour photographs of a fresh mountain stream contrasted with a stagnant pond choked with rubbish (wildlife magazines are a good source for this kind of information).

Prayer

Read a simple version of the Creation story from the Book of Genesis (The Children's Bible – Hamlyn Children's Books), or you may prefer to use prayers created by the children themselves.

ACTION RHYMES AND POEMS

WATER

(Action poem – could be sung as a round)

Row, row, row your boat
Gently down the stream
If you catch a jellyfish
Wave your arms and scream.

Row, row, row your boat
Gently round the lake,
Watch out for the crocodile
And look out for the snake.

Row, row, row your boat
Gently down the river,
If you see a polar bear
Don't forget to shiver.

Row, row, row your boat
Gently out to sea,
If you meet a big blue whale
Ask her home to tea.

Lucy Coats

DAYS BY THE SEA

Sea crashes over rocks
and runs across the strand,
and when it trickles back
it leaves my footprints, in the sand.

When I've built a lovely castle
with my bucket and my spade,
back comes the water
to break up all I've made.

There are shells in my bucket
and fish in the sea,
and time to watch the sailing boats
before we have our tea.

Tomorrow if the sun shines,
we'll be back for more,
to swim and paddle, and to play,
on the sandy sea shore.

Jan Pollard

PARK POND

The park pond sparkles
  grey and white,
In places it is mucky.

The water isn't really
  deep, it's
just halfway up the ducky.

John Rice

THE HARBOUR WALL

In winter,
when the wind is wild,
the sea's as grey
as a muddy puddle.

Then the harbour wall
curls its long arm
around the boats
bobbing in a huddle.

'Come here. I'll keep you safe,'
the wall seems to say.
And it gives the bobbing boats
a cuddle.

Wes Magee

WHO LIVES IN THE SEA?

I do says the fish,
I swim where I wish,
but I hide in the dark,
well away from the shark.
I do says the whale,
as he lifts his big tail,
while I cruise along
I sing a whale song.
I do says the seal,
I eat fish for my meal,
like the penguins I see,
as they swim around me.
I do says the crab,
with my big front claws,
I push all my food
in through my jaws.
I do says the jellyfish,
but don't come near me,
my tentacles sting,
if you swim in the sea.
I do says the octopus,
as his arms wave around.
I squirt ink on my enemies
and they soon go to ground.

Who lives in the sea?
I'm glad it's not me.

Jan Pollard

WASHDAY

I'm pushing the clothes
in the washing machine.
They're dirty now
but they'll come out clean.
(mime pushing the clothes into the front of the machine)

The clothes go round
and round and round,
with suds and bubbles
and a swishing sound.
(make circles in the air with hands to show washing going round)

I'm hanging the clothes up
one by one.
They'll dry in the breeze
and the hot, bright sun.

Lift and peg
and lift and peg,
sleeve of shirt
and trouser leg.
(lift and peg in rhythm to the words)

When they're dry
they're a tangly mess,
so I get out the iron
and give them a press.

Fold and press
and fold and press,
wrinkly shirt
and creased-up dress.
(fold with one hand, press iron along with the other)

Now it's the end
of washing-day,
so I pile up the clothes
and put them away.

Pile and pat
and pile and pat.
Close up the cupboard –
That's that!

*(mime piling and patting in rhythm, then close cupboard door, then brush
hands together in gesture of finality in time to last two beats)*

Tony Mitton

PHOTOCOPIABLE RESOURCES

BATHTIME

Brush your teeth
and scrub your knees
and let me see your neck!
Have you washed
behind your ears?
Have you done your back?

Get the tap on,
here's the soap,
here's the scrubbing brush!
There's dirt
inside that elbow,
let *me* give you a wash!

Rubbing, scrubbing
pummelling,
and Dad's as bad as Mum:
'You've got *potatoes*
in your toes
and *paintpots* on your thumb!'

It takes so long
to wash things off,
it really makes me moan.
Maybe next time
I'll speed things up
and do it on my own!

Judith Nicholls

THE CENTRAL HEATING

There's a monster haunts our house —
It's called the central heating.
From the way its stomach rumbles,
Goodness knows what it's been eating.

It wakes us up at night-time
With its gurglings and its groanings,
Its clattering and its clanging,
Its mutterings and moanings.

Mum says it lives on water,
In answer to my question.
I think that it must gulp it down
To get such indigestion!

John Foster

MELTING

Winter night.
All is white.
Morning sunshine glare.
Melting snow.
Overflow.
Puddles everywhere.

Wendy Larmont

WATER'S FOR...

Water's for..   washing, drinking
making tea,
cleaning the bath
or scrubbing me;
shining a car
or rinsing a shirt
watering tomatoes,
shifting the dirt
...my Mum says.

But I say...   paddling in wellies
or just wet feet
(puddles are good
but sea's a treat)
squirting at brothers
splashing Dad,
soaking my sister
to make her mad!
Mixing with mud
to bake a pie,
spraying the dog
or catching a fly.
Bath or puddle
sleet or rain,
let's all play
a WATER game!

Judith Nicholls

BUBBLES

Bubbles floating, lifting, dropping,
Blow them, catch them, watch them
popping.
See the colours of the rainbow
As they're dancing past the window.

Wendy Larmont

WET PLAYTIME

Splashing in the puddles
Playing in the rain
Rivers in the gutter
Pouring down the drain
Stamping with my wellies
Making raindrops fly
Home again at teatime
Feeling warm and dry

Wendy Larmont

RAIN

Pitter-patter, hear it raining?
Slow at first, then faster, faster.
Put on your raincoat.
Hold up your umbrella
Pull on your Wellingtons
And splash in the puddles.

*Children clap hands, gradually
faster and louder.
Pretend to do up buttons, open
umbrellas, put on boots.
Stamp their feet on the ground.*

Lillian McCrea

THE WATERFALL

Over rugged rocks
the
W
a
t
e
r
f
a
l
l
rumbles
and tumbles.

In winter
it groans, gasps
and grumbles.

In summer
it just whispers
and mumbles.

Wes Magee

THE GROWING RIVER

At first the river's very small,
And can't float anything at all;
But later, as it journeys on,
It's large enough to float a swan.

It grows till it can safely float
A slim canoe and then a boat;
And later still, as like as not,
It manages to float a yacht.

And presently, when really large,
It takes a steamer, then a barge.
And last it passes busy quays
And floats great ships to foreign seas.

Rodney Bennett

THE SHAPE OF WATER

Why does the bottle of water I pour
become a big puddle upon the floor?

Why won't it drop from the tap in a block
instead of a gush that gives us a shock?

Why is there never a waterless hole
left at the side of a washing up bowl?

Why does it slide like a slippery snake
into the basin, and then make a lake?

Why does it drip in the shape of a drop
then spread itself thinly when licked by a mop?

Gina Douthwaite

STORM

Above my house
the clouds are dark.
The sky is full of rain.
There's thunder deeply rumbling
and droplets on the pane.

So I shall stay inside my house
because it's dry and warm.
I'll stand beside the window
and watch the growing storm.

Tony Mitton

BLUE WELLIES,
YELLOW WELLIES

Blue wellies, yellow wellies,
green wellies, red.
You wear yours in puddles –
I wear mine in bed!

Judith Nicholls

VOICES OF WATER

*(Poem for group recitation
and musical accompaniment)*

The water in the rain says *Tick Tick Tack*
The water in the sleet says *Slush*
The water in the ice says *Crick Crick Crack*
The water in the snow says *Hush*

The water in the sink says *Slosh Slosh*
The water in the tap says *Drip*
The water in the bath says *Wash Wash*
The water in the cup says *Sip*

The water in the pool says Splish Splash
The water in the stream says Trill
The water in the sea says Crish Crash
The water in the pond...stays still.

The water in the soil says Sow, Sow
The water in the cloud says Give
The water in the plant says Grow, Grow
The water in the world says Live

*Note: This poem can be divided up into
parts, mimed or danced to, accompanied by
musical instruments or group vocal sound
effects. More simply, it can be read by a
leading 'caller', while the assembly audience
chant the response words in chorus.*

Tony Mitton

WHEN I WAS CHRISTENED

When I was christened
they held me up
and poured some water
out of a cup.

The trouble was
it fell on me,
and I and water
don't agree.

A lot of christeners
stood and listened:
I let them know
that I was christened.

David McCord

ICE LOLLIES

Freezing lips
Melting drips
Lots of licks
Lolly sticks

Wendy Larmont

STORIES

JONAH

A very long time ago there was a big city called Nineveh. It was so large that it took three days to walk from one side to the other. The people who lived there were very bad.

God decided to send someone to warn them that if they didn't behave better he would destroy their city.

He chose a man called Jonah.

Now Jonah did not want the job at all so he tried to run away. He went down to the docks and paid for a ticket to go on a ship that was going to sail that day. It was going to a place where Jonah hoped God would not find him.

While the ship was at sea, God sent a huge storm which tossed the ship about so roughly that the sailors thought it would break up.

Now, all through the storm, Jonah slept down below the deck in the hold. But the frightened sailors woke him up. 'You must help us to pray for help!' they said.

Jonah knew immediately what was wrong. 'It's my fault,' he said to them. I'm running away from God, and he's so angry with me that he's made the storm. You had better throw me into the sea.'

The sailors did not want to do this because they thought it would probably be bad luck to throw someone overboard — especially someone chosen by God. But the waves grew so large that in the end they had to do it. As soon as they threw Jonah into the water, the storm stopped.

Jonah sank down and down in the sea but he did not drown. Instead, he was suddenly swallowed by a *huge* whale sent by God. GULP!

And there he stayed, inside the whale's *enormous* tummy, for three days and nights, until the whale reached land and was sick. It threw Jonah (along with a lot of other horrible things) onto the shore.

Jonah was so happy to be safe on land that he thanked God for saving his life, even if he *was* in rather a mess.

When God told Jonah to go to Nineveh again, he did as he was told right away.

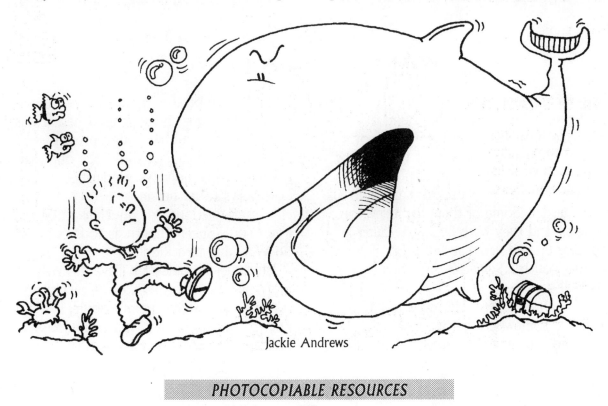

Jackie Andrews

INDOOR SPORTS

It was freezing cold in the sea. Mrs Penguin was worried.

Clive had a cough. Brenda had a sore throat.

'No swimming today,' said Mum firmly.

The penguins burst into tears. Clive had just learned to float on his back. Brenda had a new beach ball.

'We don't want to stay indoors,' they wailed.

'And I don't want you under my feet,' thought Mrs Penguin. Then she had an idea.

'There's plenty of hot water,' she said, 'You can play in the bath.'

Clive lay on his back and flapped his wings. Brenda dived for the soap. Then she fetched her ball.

Clive and Brenda had a competition – to see who could make the biggest waves.

The morning passed quickly.

'*Lunch time,*' called Mrs Penguin.

The children rushed down in bath wraps.

'Have you emptied the bath?' asked Mrs Penguin.

'Yes, Mum,' said Clive.

'Yes, Mum,' said Brenda. 'And we didn't even pull out the plug!'

Joan Stimson

WAKE UP TO A RIDDLE

Bang Bang Bang!
Mr Squelch woke up to the sound of someone hammering on his front door. He put his sleepy head out of the window. 'What is it?' he asked. 'Am I on fire?'

There were a lot of people standing in his front garden. Some of them had television cameras, and they were filming a young lady jumping up and down at the door.

'Are you Mr Squelch?' she cried excitedly.

Mr Squelch stared. He had a feeling he'd seen her somewhere before.

'Good morning, Mr Squelch. Give us a

smile! You're on the *Wakey Wakey Show!*'

Then Mr Squelch recognised her: it was Lizzie Fizz, the bubbly young presenter of his favourite breakfast show, the one that gave away free holidays. He rushed downstairs to let her in.

'Congratulations, Mr Squelch!' cried Lizzie Fizz. 'You've been chosen as today's guest on Wake Up to a Riddle!'

Mr Squelch couldn't believe it. Every morning the *Wakey Wakey Show* visited someone and asked them a riddle. If they knew the answer, they won a fabulous holiday! And today it was his turn!

'Two weeks of sunshine on a Caribbean beach could be yours, Mr Squelch, if you can work out the answer to this simple riddle. Are you ready? Here goes:

To start with I am wet and drippy;
Sometimes I am hard and nippy;
I can disappear into thin air;
You'll find me almost everywhere!
What am I?

Mr Squelch screwed up his face in concentration. 'Could you say it again?' he asked.

'I've got it written down,' said Lizzie. 'We'll leave you to have a little think, and we'll come back after lunch. Good luck!'

She handed Mr Squelch a piece of paper and rushed off down the path with everyone else following her.

Mr Squelch stared at the riddle.

'*To start with I am wet and drippy;*
Sometimes I am hard and nippy;
I can disappear into thin air;
You'll find me almost everywhere!
What am I?' he repeated slowly. 'Oh dear, oh dear. I haven't the faintest idea what it is. But I'll think about it while I have my bath.'

Mr Squelch turned the taps on. '*To start with I am wet and drippy...*' he muttered, as the water swooshed into the bath.

'Now what could that be... what in the world is wet and drippy?'

He racked his brains.

He thought and thought.

He stared out of the window.

Meanwhile, the bath filled up and up and up...

Mr Squelch was brought back to earth by the sound of dripping water and a feeling of wetness around his toes. 'ARGH!' he yelled, turning the taps off. 'That dratted riddle has made me flood the bathroom!'

It took Mr Squelch an hour to clear up the mess and get downstairs for breakfast. And he was still no nearer to answering the riddle.

'Well,' he said to himself, 'I'll just have to get on with today's little jobs, and see if it comes to me. Now, what's in the diary for this morning?'

Defrost the fridge, it said in his diary. It was certainly about time. When Mr Squelch opened the fridge door he saw it was clogged up with ice. He struggled for ages to pull the ice-cube tray out of the freezer compartment.

'Ooooh!' he cried. 'Ooooh! It's so cold. It nips your fingers!'

Mr Squelch's fingers were even more nipped as he cleared the rest of the ice from inside the fridge. Soon there was a huge pile of icy lumps on the kitchen floor beside him.

'To start with I am wet and drippy...' he muttered to himself. *'Sometimes I am cold and nippy... I don't know. What could it be?'*

He racked his brains.

He thought and thought.

He stared out of the window.

Meanwhile the pile of ice grew smaller and smaller and wetter and wetter.

Mr Squelch was brought back to earth by a feeling of wetness – very cold wetness – around his toes. 'ARGH!' he yelled. 'The ice has melted all over the floor! That dratted riddle has got me into another mess!'

It took him an hour to clear up the kitchen floor, and at the end of it he was hungry and miserable.

'Lunch time,' he said to himself. 'A nice boiled egg and soldiers. That'll cheer me up and take my mind off the riddle.'

He filled a pan with water and put in the egg to boil. But then he started thinking about the riddle again. *'I disappear into thin air... You'll find me almost everywhere...* Now what *can* it be?'

He thought and thought.

He racked his brains.

He stared out of the window.

Meanwhile, the water in the pan bubbled harder and harder. It hissed and fizzed billows of steam into the air. It bubbled down and down and down until there was no water left.

BANG! Mr Squelch was brought back to earth by the sound of a boiled egg exploding. Bits of shell and white and yolk went all over the kitchen. The bottom of the pan was burnt and black. 'ARGH!' he yelled. 'The water in the pan has boiled away! That dratted riddle has got me into a worse mess than ever.'

It took *two* hours to wash all the bits of egg off the walls and floor and ceiling *and* clean the saucepan. By the time he'd finished, Mr Squelch was in a very bad mood indeed. And he was still no nearer to solving the riddle.

Then he heard a familiar banging at the door. 'Huh!' he said. 'It's them! Those silly

people come back about their silly rhyme. Well, I'll show them!' He picked up the bucket of water he'd been using to clean the kitchen and stamped upstairs to his bedroom window. He poked his head out.

'Hello, Mr Squelch!' called Lizzie Fizz. 'Have you got the answer?'

'Huh!' said Mr Squelch. 'Your riddle has flooded my bathroom, drenched my kitchen floor and covered my house in exploded egg! *This* is my answer!'

And he emptied his bucket of water all over Lizzie Fizz's head!

'Oh,' she gasped. 'What a clever way to get it right!'

Two weeks later, as the warm Caribbean sea lapped over Mr Squelch's sunburnt toes and ice-cubes clinked in his glass of lemonade, he wondered again how he had managed to win a luxury holiday without ever solving the riddle.

But *you* know, don't you?

Sue Palmer

ELLIE'S MAGIC ROOF GARDEN

Everyone finds a new house a bit strange, but when Ellie and her Mum moved into their new house, there was one special feature which felt very weird: instead of the garden being at the back or the front, it was right at the top — almost on the roof!

They had to climb up one lot of stairs to the bedrooms. And then up another lot of stairs to the attic. And then squeeze out of a funny little door.

When they first saw the garden, there was nothing much there at all. Just a patch of concrete slabs with some rusty old buckets left around. 'We'll soon sort it out,' said Mum. 'We won't be able to have a swing out here, or a slide, but if we sit on the steps we can see as far as the edge of town and we can pretend we're right up in the sky.'

Ellie thought they were right up in the sky, because she could see people walking in the street down below, their heads bobbing along, not realising that someone was watching them. She didn't care about a swing or a slide, they weren't half as much fun.

Ellie thought the garden was a special kind of place. Magic, somehow.

Mum collected the old buckets together, cleaned them up and painted them bright colours. She made holes in the bottom of them. Then she put in bits of dishes and

stuff that had got broken when they moved and finally filled the buckets with compost from the garden centre. 'We'll plant them with lots of flowers,' Mum promised.

'Don't be silly, Mum,' said Ellie. 'Flowers grow in the ground, not in the sky!'

Mum laughed. 'We'll see about that,' she said.

On Sunday they went out to the market and bought a great many baby plants growing in pots. The market trader put them all in a large, flat box. Mum took one side and Ellie the other, and they walked slowly home carrying the box between them.

They took the plants straight up to the roof garden, two at a time. Ellie watched the heads of people passing below them.

'Wait till our plants and flowers grow,' said Mum. 'All those people will look up and smile!'

Ellie didn't believe her.

Carefully, Mum stood the plants out on the slabs. Six to each bucket. She gave Ellie a pudding spoon. 'Now you have to dig a nice little hole for each plant,' she said. Ellie dug.

Mum showed her how to knock the little plants from their pots, being careful not to crush the leaves. Then Ellie dropped them into the holes she had made and pushed the soil around them with her fingers. It felt good.

'Water next!' cried Mum. She fetched a big bowl of water out on to the roof garden. Ellie dipped her plastic watering can into the bowl to fill it and watered each of the plants carefully.

'We'll have to water them every night, now,' said Mum, 'or they will wilt and die.'

So that was what they did. Some nights they used the bath water. Some nights they used the washing up water. Some nights they used water which collected in the bowl when it rained.

Every night they touched the soil with their fingers to see how dry it was. Sometimes, after a heavy rain storm, there was no need for them to water. But this did not happen often. Mum explained that plants in buckets dried out quickly.

The plants grew and grew. They put out lots of little shoots. Mum showed Ellie how to pick out the middles to make them grow bushier.

Still Ellie watched the peoples' heads as they bobbed beneath them, but nobody ever looked up. She didn't think they would.

One day, after tea, Ellie and Mum went out on to the roof garden as usual. Everything looked the same. But Ellie could feel something was different. Something was about to happen, though she didn't know what.

She started watering the first bucket. The little tightly curled heads on the plants nodded at her as they always did. But then she noticed something she had never seen before. There were tiny cracks of different colours showing between the green leaves. Red. Gold. Pink. Orange. Purple. Blue. It was as though they were just waiting to burst open.

'They are!' laughed Mum. 'Tomorrow — you'll see!'

Ellie watered the buckets specially carefully that night. She couldn't wait to get up next morning to see what had happened.

There were flowers galore! Flowers of every colour she could think of! Flowers with their heads nodding and flowers with their faces turned up to say hello to the sun. Flowers everywhere she looked.

Down below in the street, the people stopped to point and admire. They smiled and waved to Ellie and Ellie smiled and waved back.

But that wasn't all. A few nights later, when Ellie and Mum were watering their flowers, they noticed that the lady next door was on her roof garden too, planting. And so was the man across the road, and a little boy with his dad a bit further down.

After that, people were out on their roofs every night, watering and shouting hello to each other.

And by the time the summer really arrived there were flowers growing in the sky all the way down their street. It looked so pretty that the bobbing heads looked up all the time, smiling and pointing.

And Ellie thought to herself, secretly, what a good job it was her Mum had made sure they watered their plants every night. Otherwise none of these magic gardens would have happened.

Irene Yates

PHOTOCOPIABLE RESOURCES

SONGS

WASHDAY

Guir — Rub - a - dub - a - dub — rhythm of old wash board.

Triangle — to lighten the texture.

Tambourine with jingles, as triangle rhythm.

Gillian Parker

A RAINY DAY

Splash-ing through the pud-dles as we tra-vel on our way, It's a wet, wet jour-ney in the car to-day. Switch-ing on the wi-pers to wipe a-way the spray. Lis-ten to the nois-es on a rain-y day.

Drip drip drip drip drip drip drip drip

Pit-ter pat-ter pit-ter pat-ter pit-ter pat-ter pit-ter pat-ter pit-ter pat-ter pit-ter pat-ter

Trick-le trick-le trick-le trick-le

Swish swish swish swish

drip drip drip drip

pit-ter pat-ter pit-ter pat-ter pit-ter pat-ter pit-ter pat-ter

Trick-le trick-le trick-le trick-le

Swish swish swish swish swish swish swish swish

cresc.

Lesley Funge

A MAN WITH A WATERING CAN

Quite quickly

1. Deep, deep down in the dark, dark ground, Lit- tle seed lies in the earth so brown. A -
long comes a man with a wat- er- ing can and the green shoots start to grow, grow, grow.

2. Up, up, up from the brown, brown mud,
little shoot grows to the sky above.
Along comes a man with a little watering can
and the green leaves start to grow, grow, grow.

3. Out, out, out from the green, green shoot,
little bud grows full of fruit, fruit, fruit.
Along comes a man with a watering can
and the fruit begins to grow, grow, grow.

Clive Barnwell

ONE LITTLE DROP OF WATER

One lit- tle drop of wat- er run- ning down my win- dow. When it
gets to the bot- tom it has to stop but it does- n't real- ly mat- ter there's an- oth- er at the top.

Clive Barnwell

HELLO ME!

*✷ Ask the children for more facial expressions,
for example: smiling, laughing, frowning, giggling.*

Dm

Solo: Whose is that face in the wa - ter ✷star - ing back at me?

Dm   **A7 Dm**

It looks ve - ry ve - ry like me, just who can it be?

G   **D**   **A7**   **D**

Whose is that face in the wa - ter?
Echo by the class: Whose is that face in the wat - er?

G   **D**   **A7**   **D**

It looks just like Hey. That's me!
It looks just like That's you!

Peter Morrell

I THINK ICE IS NICE

With a swing

C Am Dm G   **C Am Dm G**

1. I think ice is nice to slide a - round and I think ice is nice to glide a - round. You

E7   **Am**   **Dm G C**

touch it and it's oh so cold. Much too slip - per - y to hold.

2. I think snow is fun to run around and
I think snow is fun so come around.
We'll roll it in a great big ball.
Build a snowman oh so tall.

Debbie Campbell

WHAT'S THAT BOBBING IN THE SEA?

Chorus: **Verse:**

Sit - ting on the sand, hap - py as can be, What's that bob - bing, bob - bing in the sea? 1. It's a

lob - ster, lob - ster, Bob - bing in the sea, lob - ster, lob - ster, bob - bing in the sea.

Lob - ster, lob - ster, bob - bing in the sea, And the waves brought the lob - ster bob - bing up to me.

2. some seaweed
3. an octopus
4. a seashell
5. a jellyfish

Ann Bryant

TERRORS OF THE SEA

Bold and dan - ger - ous. No - one strange as us sail - ing out on the migh - ty sea.
Brave and dar - ing and ne - ver car - ing we're pir - ates bold like we ought to be.

Skull and cross - bones fly - ing from the flag - poles lets them know we're ter - rors of the sea.
Lots of plea - sure tak - ing peo - ple's treas - ure lets them know we're ter - rors of the sea.

Clive Barnwell

MY LITTLE ISLAND

D ... **A7** ... **D**

Here I am on my lit-tle is-land, My lit-tle is-land, My lit-tle is-land.

A7 ... **D**

Here I am on my lit-tle is-land, Guess what I'm do-ing here? 1. I'm

G ... **D** ... **Em** ... **C** ... **D**

mak-ing a fire, Mak-ing a fire, Mak-ing a fire on my lit-tle is-land.

G ... **D** ... **A7** ... **D**

Mak-ing a fire, Mak-ing a fire, That's what I'm do-ing here.

2. I'm catching a fish...
3. I'm cooking the fish...
4. I'm eating the fish...
5. I'm going to sleep...

Ann Bryant

THEMES
for early years

Name _____

What's the weather?

sunny

cloudy

rain

snow

lightning

wind (direction)

THEMES
for early years

Name _____

How many?

◆ How many icy things are there in each picture?

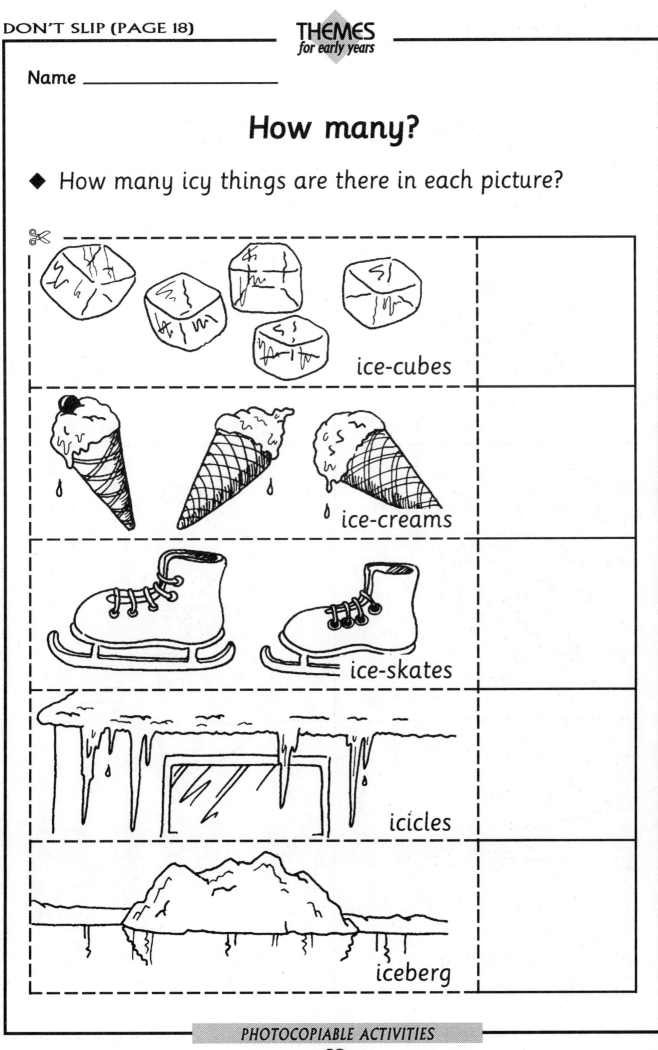

ice-cubes

ice-creams

ice-skates

icicles

iceberg

THEMES
for early years

Name ⎯⎯⎯⎯⎯⎯⎯⎯⎯⎯

Anchor the boat

◆ Join each boat to its anchor.

Reflections

◆ Place a mirror along the edge of each shape.
Draw in the other half of the shape.

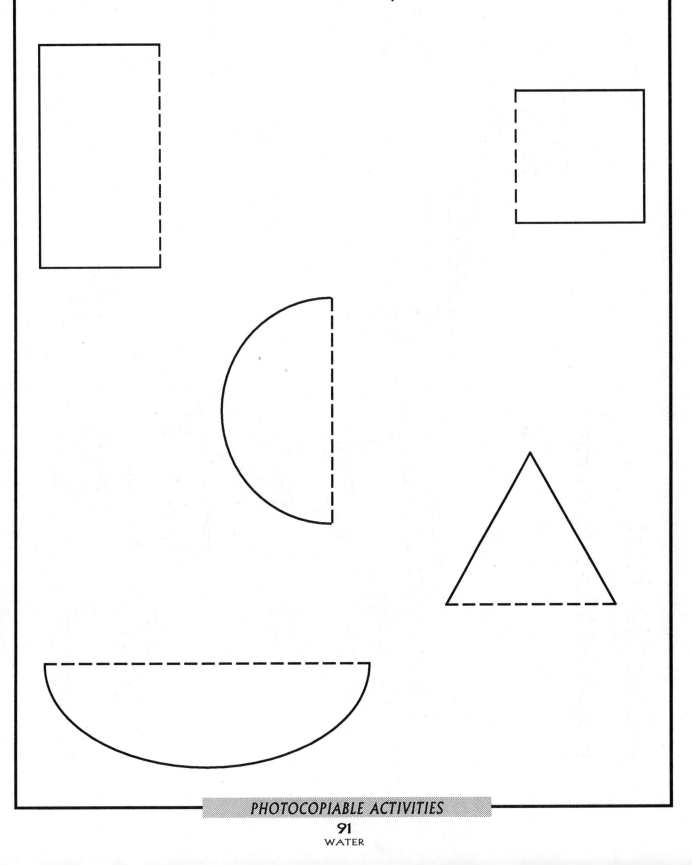

Name _____

Washing

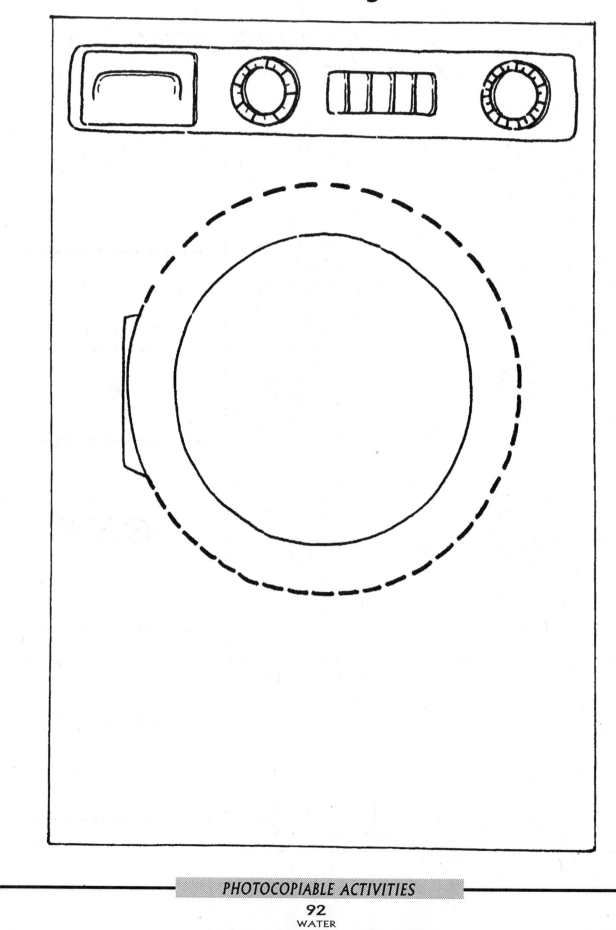

Name _____

Flappers and flippers

◆ Write in the small box the first letter of the bird's name. Then finish the pictures of the birds.

penguin

_____

duck

_____

heron

_____

swan

_____

THEMES *for early years*

Name _____

Catch a fish

end

start→

THEMES
for early years

Name _____

Which position?

◆ Put your counters in the right place.

diver

treasure

submarine

oyster

jellyfish

octopus

cave

sponge

RECOMMENDED MATERIALS

MUSIC AND SONGS

Apusskidu : 56 Songs for Children (A&C Black)
Knock At The Door Jan Betts (Ward Lock)
Okki-tokki-unga (A&C Black)
Oranges and Lemons compiled by Karen King (OUP) and tape of party games
Round and Round the Garden Sarah Williams (OUP) and tape of 40 play rhymes
Someone's Singing Lord (A&C Black)
Ta-ra-ra boom-de-ay (A&C Black)
The Funny Family (Ward Lock)
Up, up and away Derek Pearson (OUP)

POEMS AND RHYMES

A Child's Garden Of Verses Robert Louis Stevenson (Wordsworth)
Now We Are Six A. A. Milne (Methuen)
Sea Poems compiled by John Foster (OUP)
The Book of a Thousand Poems (Collins)
The Oxford Nursery Rhyme Book assembled by Iona and Peter Opie
The Young Puffin Book of Verse compiled by Barbara Ireson (Out of print)
This Little Puffin, compiled by Elizabeth Matterson
Water Poems compiled by John Foster (OUP)
When We Were Very Young A A Milne (Methuen)

PICTURE AND STORY BOOKS

Fables Aesop and Jacqueline Morley (Macdonald)
Bible Story Book Georgie Adams (Orion)
Bodkin Keeper of the Marsh Nick Hesketh (Amaising Publishing)
Fireman Sam Caroline Hill-Trevor (Buzz Books – Reed International)
Gumdrop and the Pirates Val Biro (Puffin)
I can cook Sarah Maxwell (Lorenz)
I Love Boats Flora McDonnell (Walker Books)
Mr Archimedes' Bath Pamela Allen (Puffin)
Mrs Mopple's Washing Line Anita Hewett (Random House)
Mrs Plug the Plumber Allan Ahlberg (Young Puffin) and cassette
Peter Pan Ladybird Disney
Rain, Hail or Shine Nan Hunt (Collins/Angus and Robertson)
Six Folk Tales adapted by Sheila Lane and Marion Kemp from *Folk Tales* by Leila Berg (Ward Lock)
Skeleton Crew Allan Ahlberg (Mammoth)

The Lion Storyteller Bible
The Princess and the Pea Fairy Tale series (Michael O'Mara Books)
The Three Railway Engines The Rev. W. Awdry (Heinemann)
The Tunnel Brian Wildsmith (OUP)
Wet World Norma Simon (Walker Books)
Who's in the Deep Blue Sea? Peter Seymour (Child's Play International)

INFORMATION BOOKS

Children's Encyclopaedia Britannica
Discovering Oceans, Lakes, Ponds, and Puddles Jerome Ashford Frame (Lion)
Discovering the Four Seasons Jeffery Scott Wallace (Lion)
Down by the Drains Barbara James (Wayland)
Floating and Sinking Kay Davies and Wendy Oldfield (Wayland)
I Wonder Why the Sea is Salty Anita Ganerie (Kingfisher)
National Trust Book of Forgotten Household Crafts John Seymour (Dorling Kindersley)
The Pond Nathalie Tordjman (Moonlight)
The Wonder of Water Bonita Searle-Barnes (Lion)

ADDRESSES AND OTHER RESOURCES

'The way of Islam poster set', includes a poster of the Muslim ritual washing ceremony of wudu. This can be obtained from: Religion in Evidence, Technology Teaching Systems Ltd, Unit 7, Monk Road, Alfreton, Derbyshire DE55 7RL.
Religion in Evidence also provides a book of nursery rhymes which are based on traditional English rhymes but cover Muslim beliefs – *Muslim Nursery Rhymes.*
The RNLI for the young is at: Storm Force HQ RNLI, West Quay Road, Poole, Dorset BH15 1HZ.
The Amazing World of Water, North West Water Ltd, Lingley Mere, Great Sankey, Warrington WA5 3LQ.
Many toys, games and equipment are stocked by Early Learning Centres such as:
Aquaplay – a canal system with a paddle wheel to start the water flowing; Bubble Beater – wind the handle to create bubbles, whirlpools and waves; Catch and Count – a fishing game; Play sink set – can let water in and out.